Starting a Business FOR DUMMIES® PORTABLE EDITION

by Colin Barrow

WILEY

A John Wiley and Sons, Ltd, Publication

Starting a Business For Dummies, Portable Edition
Published by
John Wiley & Sons, Ltd
The Atrium
Southern Gate
Chichester
West Sussex
PO19 8SQ
England

E-mail (for orders and customer service enquires): cs-books@wiley.co.uk

Visit our Home Page on www.wiley.com

For general information on our other products and services, please contact our Customer Care Department within the U.S. at 877-762-2974, outside the U.S. at 317-572-3993, or fax 317-572-4002.

For technical support, please visit www.wiley.com/techsupport.

Wiley also publishes its books in a variety of electronic formats. Some content that appears in print may not be available in electronic books.

British Library Cataloguing in Publication Data: A catalogue record for this book is available from the British Library.

ISBN: 978-1-119-97440-6 (paperback), ISBN: 978-1-119-97484-0 (ebk),

ISBN: 978-1-119-97485-7 (ebk), ISBN: 978-1-119-97486-4 (ebk)

Printed and bound in Great Britain by TJ International, Padstow, Cornwall

10 9 8 7 6 5 4 3 2 1

WILEY

About the Author

Colin Barrow was, until recently, Head of the Enterprise Group at Cranfield School of Management, where he taught entrepreneurship on the MBA and other programmes. He is also a visiting professor at business schools in the US, Asia, France, and Austria. His books on entrepreneurship and small business have been translated into twenty languages including Russian and Chinese. He worked with Microsoft to incorporate the business planning model used in his teaching programmes into the software program, Microsoft Business Planner. He is a regular contributor to newspapers, periodicals and academic journals such as the *Financial Times, The Guardian, Management Today*, and the *International Small Business Journal*.

Thousands of students have passed through Colin's start-up and business growth programmes, going on to run successful and thriving enterprises, and raising millions in new capital. He is on the board of several small businesses, is a University Academic Governor, and has served on the boards of public companies, venture capital funds, and on Government Task Forces.

Author's Acknowledgments

I would like to thank everyone at Wiley for the opportunity to write and update this book – as well as for their help, encouragement, feedback, and tireless work to make this all happen.

Publisher's Acknowledgments

We're proud of this book; please send us your comments through our Dummies online registration form located at www.dummies.com/register/.

Some of the people who helped bring this book to market include the following:

Acquisitions, Editorial, and Media Development

Project Editor: Jo Jones

Commissioning Editor: Samantha Spickernell

Assistant Editor: Ben Kemble

Development Editor: Sally Lansdell

Proofreader: Charlie Wilson

Production Manager: Daniel Mersey

Publisher: David Palmer

Cover Photos: ©Picsfive

Cartoons: Ed McLachlan

Composition Services

Project Coordinator: Kristie Rees

Layout and Graphics: Melanee Habig

Proofreader: Rebecca Denoncour

Indexer: Potomac Indexing, LLC

Contents at a Glance

Table of Contents

Introduction

*I*f you've pulled this book down from the shelf or had it passed to you by a friend or loved one as a gift, you don't have to be psychic to know something about your current business situation. You may be in need of this book for any number of reasons:

- ✔ You saw Lehman Brothers' staff queuing outside their offices with cardboard boxes and don't want that to happen to your business.

- ✔ A relative, hopefully a distant and elderly one, has died and left you a pile of dosh and you don't fancy leaving it to your stockbroker to lose on your behalf.

- ✔ Your employer is in the middle of a major downsizing operation as well as proposing to close its final salary pension scheme and relocate to somewhere with lousy schools and no healthcare facilities.

- ✔ You have a great idea for a world-beating product that no one has ever thought of but every one of the world's billion Internet users desperately needs – when they hear the good news they're going to click a path to your website.

- ✔ Your brother, sister, father, mother or best friend – or worse still, all of them – has started his or her own business and retired to a chateau in France to breed horses, tend the vines and sail on a luxury yacht.

If your present situation is founded largely on luck and serendipity, that isn't enough to get you through the business start-up process unaided. Good ideas, hard work, relevant skills and knowledge about your product and its market, though essential, on their own aren't enough. The 400,000 small firms that close their doors every year in the United Kingdom, a figure that rose sharply in the recent recession, are evidence enough that the process is a tough one.

This icon calls your attention to particularly important points and offers useful advice on practical topics.

This icon serves as a friendly reminder that the topic at hand is important enough for you to make a note of.

Business, like any specialist subject, is awash with specialised terms and expressions, some of which may not be familiar to you. This icon draws your attention to these.

This icon alerts you that I'm using a practical example showing how another business starter has tackled a particular topic. Often you can apply the example to your own business.

This icon alerts you to a potential danger. Proceed with caution; look left and right before crossing. In fact, think carefully about crossing at all when you see this icon.

This icon refers to specialised business facts and data that are interesting as background data but not essential for you to know. You can skip paragraphs marked by this icon without missing the point – but reading them may help you build credibility with outside investors and partners.

Where to Go From Here

Take a minute to thumb through the table of contents and get comfortable with the topics the book covers. Pick a chapter that strikes a particular chord with the aspect of starting a business that's uppermost in your mind. Read that and see where it leads you.

You can also use Chapter 6, 'Preparing the Business Plan', as a framework for gathering knowledge and diving back into the other chapters as you go.

If all else fails, start at the beginning. That technique has a pretty good track record.

Part I
Getting Started

'OK – Here's the business plan. Nigel takes charge of marketing, Tristram sales, Keith accounts and Psycho makes sure clients pay on time.'

In this part . . .

Before you can think seriously about starting your own business, you need to make sure you're ready for such a big step. This part lets you check out your skills and aptitude and see how they compare to the business idea you have in mind. You can see if your idea looks able to make the kind of money you're expecting. Then check if you should start up on your own or perhaps find others to help you.

Once you've done the groundwork you can start investigating the market in more detail and lay the groundwork for opening your doors for business either at home or in dedicated premises. With this work done you are ready to take your business forward!

Chapter 1

Preparing for Business

• •

In This Chapter

▶ Getting to grips with the basics of business strategy

▶ Working up to opening up

▶ Measuring your business's viability

▶ Growing for success

• •

*W*hen you're starting a business, particularly your first business, you need to carry out the same level of preparation as you would for crossing the Gobi Desert or exploring the jungles of South America. You're entering hostile territory.

Your business idea may be good, it may even be great, but such ideas are two a penny. The patent office is stuffed full of great inventions that have never returned tuppence to the inventors who spent so much time and money filing them. It's how you plan, how you prepare and how you implement your plan that makes the difference between success and failure. And failure is pretty much a norm for business start-ups. Tens of thousands of small firms fail, some disastrously, every year. Most are perfectly ordinary enterprises – catastrophe isn't confined to brash Internet whiz kids entering markets a decade or so ahead of the game.

This chapter sets the scene to make sure that you're well prepared for the journey ahead.

Understanding the Enduring Rules of Business Strategy

When you're engulfed by enthusiasm for an idea for a new business or engaged in the challenge of getting it off the ground you can easily miss out on the knowledge you can gain by lifting your eyes up and taking the big picture on board too. There isn't much point in taking aim at the wrong target from the outset!

Credit for devising the most succinct and usable way to get a handle on the big picture has to be given to Michael E. Porter, who trained as an economist at Princeton, taking his MBA at Harvard Business School where he's now a professor. Porter's research led him to conclude that two factors above all influence a business's chances of making superior profits – surely an absolute must if you're going to all the pain of working for yourself.

- ✔ **The attractiveness or otherwise of the industry in which it primarily operates.** That's down to your research, a subject I cover later in this book.

- ✔ **How the business positions itself within the industry in terms of an organisation's sphere of influence.** In that respect a business can only have a cost advantage if it can make products or deliver services for less than others. Or the business may be different in a way that matters to consumers, so that its offers are unique, or at least relatively so.

Porter added a further twist to his prescription. Businesses can follow either a cost advantage path or a differentiation path industry wide, or they can take a third path – they can concentrate on a narrow specific segment either with cost advantage or differentiation. This he termed *focus strategy*, which I discuss in the following sections.

Focus, focus, focus

Whoa up a minute. Before you can get a handle on focus you need to understand exactly what the good professor means by *cost leadership* and *differentiation*, because the combination of those provides the most fruitful arena for a new business to compete.

Cost leadership

Don't confuse low cost with low price. A business with low costs may or may not pass those savings on to customers. Alternatively, the business could use low costs alongside tight cost controls and low margins to create an effective barrier to others considering either entering or extending their penetration of that market.

Businesses are most likely to achieve low cost strategies in large markets, requiring large-scale capital investment, where production or service volumes are high and businesses can achieve economies of scale from long runs. If you have deep pockets, or can put together a proposition that convinces the money men to stump up the cash, this could be an avenue to pursue.

Ryanair and easyJet are examples of fairly recent business start-ups where analysing every component of the business made it possible to strip out major elements of cost – meals, free baggage and allocated seating, for example – while leaving the essential proposition – we will fly you from A to B – intact. Enough of a strategy to give bigger, more established rivals such as British Airways a few sleepless nights.

Differentiation

The key to *differentiation* (making sure your product or service has a unique element that makes it stand out from the rest) is a deep understanding of what customers really want and need and more importantly what they're prepared to pay more for. Apple's opening strategy was based around a 'fun' operating system based on icons, rather than the dull MS-DOS. This belief was based on Apple's understanding that computer users were mostly young and wanted an intuitive command system and the 'graphical user interface' delivered just that. Apple has continued its differentiation strategy, but added design and fashion to ease of control to the ways in which it delivers extra value. Sony and BMW and are also examples of differentiators. Both have distinctive and desirable differences in their products and neither they nor Apple offer the lowest price in their respective industries; customers are willing to pay extra for the idiosyncratic and prized differences embedded in their products.

Consumers can be a pretty fickle bunch. Just dangle something faster, brighter or just plain newer and you can usually grab their attention. Your difference doesn't have to be profound or even high-tech to capture a slice of the market. Book buyers rushed in droves to Waterstone's for no more profound a reason than that its doors remained open in the evenings and on Sundays, when most other established bookshops were firmly closed.

Focus

Your patience is about to be rewarded. Now I can get to the strategy that Porter reckoned was the most fruitful for new business starters to plunge into.

Focused strategy involves concentrating on serving a particular market or a defined geographic region. IKEA, for example, targets young, white collar workers as its prime customer segment, selling through 235 stores in more than 30 countries. Ingvar Kamprad, an entrepreneur from the Småland province in southern Sweden, who founded the business in the late 1940s, offers home furnishing products of good function and design at prices young people can afford. He achieves this by using simple cost-cutting solutions that don't affect the quality of products.

Warren Buffett, the world's richest man, knows a thing or two about focus. His investment company combined with Mars to buy US chewing gum manufacturer Wrigley for $23 billion (£11.6 billion) in May 2008. Chigago-based Wrigley, which launched its Spearmint and Juicy Fruit gums in the 1890s, has specialised in chewing gum ever since and consistently outperformed its more diversified competitors. Wrigley is the only major consumer products company to grow comfortably faster than the population in its markets and above the rate of inflation. Over the past decade or so, for example, other consumer products companies have diversified. Gillette moved into batteries used to drive many of its products by acquiring Duracell. Nestlé bought Ralston Purina, Dreyer's, Ice Cream Partners and Chef America. Both have trailed Wrigley's performance.

Recognising the first-to-market fallacy

People use the words 'first mover advantage' like a mantra to justify a headlong rush into starting a business without doing enough basic research. That won't happen to you – after all, you're reading this book and by the end of this section you'll be glad you paused for thought.

The idea that you have the best chance of being successful if you get in first is one of the most enduring in business theory and practice. Entrepreneurs and established giants are always in a race to be first. Research from the 1980s claimed to show that market pioneers have enduring advantages in distribution, product-line breadth, product quality and, especially, market share.

Beguiling though the theory of first mover advantage is, it's probably wrong. Gerard Tellis, of the University of Southern California, and Peter Golder, of New York University's Stern Business School, argue in their research that previous studies on the subject were deeply flawed. In the first instance earlier studies were based on surveys of surviving companies and brands, excluding all the pioneers that failed. This helps some companies to look as though they were first to market even when they weren't. Procter & Gamble boasts that it created America's disposable-nappy (diaper) business. In fact a company called Chux launched its product a quarter of a century before Procter & Gamble entered the market in 1961.

Also, the questions used to gather much of the data in earlier research were at best ambiguous and perhaps dangerously so. For example, researchers had used the term 'one of the pioneers in first developing such products or services' as a proxy for 'first to market'. The authors emphasise their point by listing popular misconceptions of who the real pioneers were across the 66 markets they analysed:

- ✔ **Online book sales:** Amazon (wrong); Books.com (right).

- ✔ **Copiers:** Xerox (wrong); IBM (right).

- ✔ **PCs:** IBM/Apple (both wrong); Micro Instrumentation Telemetry Systems (right) – it introduced its PC, the Altair, a $400 kit, in 1974 followed by Tandy Corporation (Radio Shack) in 1977.

In fact the most compelling evidence from all the research is that nearly half of all firms pursuing a first to market strategy are fated to fail, but those following fairly close behind are three times as likely to succeed. Tellis and Golder claim the best strategy is to enter the market a few years after pioneers, learn from their mistakes, benefit from their product and market development and be more certain about customer preferences.

Getting in Shape to Start Up

You need to be in great shape to start a business. You don't have to diet or exercise, at least not in the conventional sense of those words, but you do have to be sure that you have the skills and knowledge you need for the business you have in mind, or know how to tap into sources of such expertise.

The following sections help you through a pre-opening check-up so that you can be absolutely certain that your abilities and interests are closely aligned to those that the business you have in mind requires. The sections also help you to check that a profitable market exists for your products or services. You can use these sections as a vehicle for sifting through your business ideas to see whether they're worth the devotion of time and energy that you need to start up a business.

Assessing your abilities

Business lore claims that for every ten people who want to start their own business, only one finally does. It follows that an awful lot of dreamers exist who, while liking the idea of starting their own business, never get around to taking action. See whether you fit into one of the following entrepreneurial categories:

- ✔ **Nature:** If one of your parents or siblings runs their own business, successfully or otherwise, you're highly likely to start up your own business. No big surprise here, as the rules and experiences of business are being discussed every day and some of it's bound to rub off. It also helps if you're a risk taker who's comfortable with uncertainty.

- ✔ **Nurture:** For every entrepreneur whose parents or siblings have a business there are two who don't. If you can find a business idea that excites you and has the prospect of providing personal satisfaction and wealth, then you can assemble all the skills and resources needed to succeed in your own business. You need to acquire good planning and organisational skills and either develop a well-rounded knowledge of basic finance, people management, operational systems, business law, marketing and selling, or get help and advice from people who have that knowledge.

✔ **Risk taker:** If you crave certainty in everything you do, then running your own business may be something of a culture shock. By the time the demand for a product or service is an absolutely sure-fire thing, there may already be too many other businesses in the market to leave much room for you. Don't confuse risk taking with a pure gamble. You need to be able to weigh matters up and make your risk a calculated one.

✔ **Jack-of-all-trades:** You need to be prepared to do any business task at any time. The buck definitely stops with you when you run your own business. You can't tell a customer that his delivery is late just because a driver fails to show up. You just have to put in a few more hours and do the job yourself.

Discovering a real need

You may be a great potential entrepreneur, but you still need to spell out exactly what it is you plan to do, who needs it and how it can make money. A good starting point is to look around and see whether anyone is dissatisfied with their present suppliers. Unhappy customers are fertile ground for new businesses to work in.

One dissatisfied customer isn't enough to start a business for. Make sure that unhappiness is reasonably widespread, because that gives you a feel for how many customers may be prepared to defect. After you have an idea of the size of the potential market, you can quickly see whether your business idea is a money-making proposition.

Aside from asking around, one way to get a handle on dissatisfaction levels is to check out websites that allow consumers to register their feelings, such as www.complaints.com, www.grumbletext.co.uk and www.blagger.com. Then scour blogs (short for weblogs), where irate people can complain their hearts out. Check out websites such as www.technorati.com, www.totalblogdirectory.com and www.bloghub.com, which all operate blog-indexing services that can help you filter through the 70 million plus blogs and reach the few dozen that serve the sector you're interested in.

The easiest way to fill a need that people are going to pay to have satisfied is to tap into one or more of these triggers:

✓ **Cost reduction and economy:** Anything that saves customers money is always an attractive proposition. Lastminute.com's appeal is that it acts as a 'warehouse' for unsold hotel rooms and airline tickets that you can have at a heavy discount.

✓ **Fear and security:** Products that protect customers from any danger, however obscure, are enduringly appealing. When Long-Term Capital Management (LTCM), one of America's largest hedge funds, collapsed and had to be rescued by the Federal Reserve at a cost of $2 billion, it nearly brought down the American financial system single-handedly. Two months later Ian and Susan Jenkins launched the first issue of their magazine, *EuroHedge*. At the time 35 hedge funds existed in Europe, but investors knew little about them and were rightly fearful for their investments. *EuroHedge* provided information and protection to a nervous market and five years after its launch the Jenkinses sold the magazine for £16.5 million.

✓ **Greed:** Anything that offers the prospect of making exceptional returns is always a winner.

✓ **Niche markets:** Big markets are usually the habitat of big business – encroach on their territory at your peril. New businesses thrive in markets that are too small even to be an appetite whetter to established firms. These market niches are often easy prey to new entrants because businesses have usually neglected, ignored or served them badly in the past.

Checking the fit of the business

Having a great business idea and possessing the attributes and skills you require to start your own business successfully are two vital elements to get right before you launch. The final ingredient is to be sure that the business you plan to start is right for you.

Before you go too far, make an inventory of the key things that you're looking for in a business. These may include working hours that suit your lifestyle; the opportunity to meet new people; minimal paperwork; a chance to travel. Then match those up with the proposition you're considering.

Confirming Viability

An idea, however exciting, unique, revolutionary and necessary, isn't a business. It's a great starting point, and an essential one, but you have to do a good deal more work before you can sidle up to your boss and tell him exactly what you think of him.

The following sections explore the steps you need to take so that you don't have to go back to your boss in six months and plead for your old job back (and possibly eat a large piece of humble pie at the same time).

Researching the market

However passionate you are about your business idea, you're unlikely already to have the answers to all the important questions concerning your marketplace. Before you can develop a successful business strategy, you have to understand as much as possible about your market and the competitors you're likely to face.

The main way to get to understand new business areas, or areas that are new to you at any rate, is to conduct market research. The purpose of that research is to ensure that you have sufficient information on customers, competitors and markets so that your market entry strategy or expansion plan is at least on target, if not on the bull's-eye itself. In other words, you need to explore whether enough people are attracted to buy what you want to sell at a price that gives you a viable business. If you miss the target altogether, which you may well do without research, you may not have the necessary resources for a second shot.

The areas to research include:

- ✔ **Your customers:** Who may buy more of your existing goods and services and who may buy your new goods and services? How many such customers exist? What particular customer needs do you meet?

- ✔ **Your competitors:** Who are you competing with in your product/market areas? What are those firms' strengths and weaknesses?

✔ **Your product or service:** How can you tailor your product or service to meet customer needs and give you an edge in the market?

✔ **The price:** What do customers see as giving value for money, so encouraging both loyalty and referral?

✔ **The advertising and promotional material:** What newspapers, journals and so forth do your potential customers read and what websites do they visit? Unglamorous as it is, analysing data on what messages actually influence people to buy, rather than just to click, holds the key to identifying where and how to promote your products and service.

✔ **Channels of distribution:** How can you get to your customers and who do you need to distribute your products or services? You may need to use retailers, wholesalers, mail order or the Internet. These methods all have different costs and if you use one or more, each wants a slice of your margin.

✔ **Your location:** Where do you need to be to reach your customers most easily at minimum cost? Sometimes you don't actually need to be anywhere near your market, particularly if you anticipate most of your sales coming from the Internet. If this is the case you need to have a strategy to make sure that potential customers can find your website.

 Try to spend your advertising money wisely. Nationwide advertisements or blanketing the market with free CD-ROMs may create huge short-term growth, but little evidence exists that indiscriminate blunderbuss advertising works well in retaining customers. Certainly, few people using such techniques make any money.

Doing the numbers

Your big idea looks as though it has a market. You've evaluated your skills and inclinations and you believe that you can run this business. The next crucial question is – can it make you money?

You absolutely must establish the financial viability of your idea before you invest money in it or approach outsiders for backing. You need to carry out a thorough appraisal of the business's financial requirements. If the numbers come out as unworkable, you can then rethink your business proposition without losing anything. If the figures look good, then you can go ahead and prepare cash flow projections, a profit and loss account and a balance sheet, and put together the all-important business plan.

You need to establish for your business:

- ✔ Day-to-day operating costs
- ✔ How long it will take to reach break-even
- ✔ How much start-up capital you need
- ✔ The likely sales volume
- ✔ The profit level you require for the business not just to survive, but also to thrive
- ✔ The selling price of your product or service

Many businesses have difficulty raising start-up capital. To compound this, one of the main reasons small businesses fail in the early stages is that they use too much start-up capital to buy fixed assets. Although some equipment is clearly essential at the start, you can postpone other purchases. You may be better off borrowing or hiring 'desirable' and labour-saving devices for a specific period. This obviously isn't as nice as having them to hand all the time, but remember that you have to maintain and perhaps update every photocopier, printer, computer and delivery van you buy and they become part of your fixed costs. The higher your fixed costs, the longer it usually takes to reach break-even point and profitability. And time isn't usually on the side of the small, new business: it has to become profitable relatively quickly or it simply runs out of money and dies.

Raising the money

Two fundamentally different types of money that a business can tap into are debt and equity.

- ✔ **Debt** is money borrowed, usually from a bank, and that you have to repay. While you're making use of borrowed money you also have to pay interest on the loan.

✔ **Equity** is the money that shareholders, including the pro-prietor, put in and money left in the business by way of retained profit. You don't have to give the shareholders their money back, but shareholders do expect the directors to increase the value of their shares, and if you go public they'll probably expect a stream of dividends too.

If you don't meet the shareholders' expectations, they won't be there when you need more money – or, if they're powerful enough, they'll take steps to change the membership of the board.

Alternative financing methods include raising money from family and friends, applying for grants and awards, and entering business competitions.

The Financial Services Authority, a City watchdog, ordered all banks to publish statistics on complaints on their website from 31 August 2010. Lloyds had received 288,717 complaints in the first six months of the year, Santander 244,978, Barclays 195,956 and HSBC had just 65,236.

Writing up the business plan

A *business plan* is a selling document that conveys the excite-ment and promise of your business to potential backers and stakeholders. These potential backers can include bankers, venture capital firms, family, friends and others who may help you launch your business if they only know what you want to do.

Getting money is expensive, time consuming and hard work. Having said that, you can get a quick decision. One recent start-up succeeded in raising £3 million in eight days, after the founder turned down an earlier offer of £1 million made just 40 minutes after he presented his business plan. Your busi-ness plan should cover what you expect to achieve over the next three years.

Chapter 2

Doing the Groundwork

• •

In This Chapter

▶ Understanding what a small business is

▶ Checking whether you're the business type

▶ Running towards great ideas and avoiding bad ones

▶ Appreciating the impact of the broader economy

▶ Recognising success characteristics

• •

*I*f you've worked in a big organisation, you know that a small and medium enterprise (SME) is a very different kind of animal from a big business. SMEs are more vulnerable to the vagaries of the economy, but are vital to its vigour.

In this chapter you can find out how to come up with a great business idea and avoid the lemons. You can also look at the most common mistakes that businesses starting up make and how you can avoid them.

Understanding the Small Business Environment

During one of the all too many periods in recent history when the business climate was particularly frigid, the recent global credit crunch being a good example, some bright spark claimed that the only sure-fire way to get a small business safely down the slipway was to start out with a big one and shrink it down to size. There's no denying that's one way to get started, but even as a joke the statement completely misses the point. Small businesses have almost nothing in common with big ones. Just because someone, you perhaps, has worked in a big business, however successfully, that's no guarantee of success in the small business world.

Big businesses usually have deep pockets and even if those pockets aren't actually stuffed full of cash, after years of trading under their belt they can in all but the most extraordinary of circumstances get the ear of their bank manager. Even if unsuccessful at the bank big firms can generally extract credit from suppliers, especially if the suppliers are smaller and susceptible to being lent on in order to retain them as a customer. If all else fails big businesses may have the option to tap their shareholders or go out to the stock market for more boodle – options a small business owner can only dream about. And of course if the business is very big, in times of extreme hardship it can expect a sympathetic hearing from the government.

In contrast, small business founders have to stay up late burning the midnight oil, poring over those figures themselves. To cap it all, they may even have to get up at dawn and make special deliveries to customers in order to ensure that they meet deadlines.

Looking at the Types of People Who Start Businesses

At one level statistics on small firms are very precise. Government collects and analyses the basic data on how many businesses start (and close) in each geographic area and what type of activity those businesses undertake. Periodic studies give further insights into how new and small firms are financed or how much of their business comes from overseas markets. Beyond that the 'facts' become a little more hazy and information comes most often from informal studies by banks, academics and others who may have a particular axe to grind.

The first fact about the UK small business sector is how big it is. Over 4.7 million people now run their own business, up from 1.9 million some three decades ago.

The desire to start a business isn't evenly distributed across the population as a whole. Certain factors such as geographic area and age group seem to influence the number of start-ups at any one time. The following sections explore some of these factors.

Making your age an asset

Research by the Global Entrepreneurship Monitor (www. gemconsortium.org) and the UK Office for National Statistics (www.statistics.gov.uk) reveals a number of interesting facts about small business starters. First, people aged between 25 and 44 are more likely than those in other age groups to be planning to start a business. Over 5 per cent of people in the 25–44 age group are starting a business on their own or with others. Around 3 per cent of those under 24 or between 45 and 54 also have business start-up plans. Those over 55 are the least likely to want to start up, with only 1.5 per cent heading for self-employment.

But those percentages are only showing those planning a start-up. Around three times those proportions are already running small or medium-sized businesses.

Considering location

More than three times as many people in London start a business as do those in the North East of England. At the very least you're more likely to feel lonelier as an entrepreneur in that area, or in Wales and Scotland, than in, say, London or the South East.

According to the UK Office for National Statistics the chances of your business surviving are best in Northern Ireland, where just over 70 per cent are still going after three years, and worst in London, where around 60 per cent of businesses remain after three years.

Select Database, a direct marketing firm, has a nifty database that can tell you how many businesses have been set up recently in any postal district in the UK (www.selectabase. co.uk/startupsplus).

Winning with women

Women in Europe currently own less than a third of small businesses, but women start about 35 per cent of new businesses in the UK. Businesses started by women tend to be concentrated in the labour-intensive retail industries, where management skills are particularly valuable.

The British Association of Women Entrepreneurs (www.bawe-uk.org) and Everywoman (www.everywoman.co.uk) are useful starting points to find out more about targeted help and advice for women starting up a business.

Self-employment, a term used interchangeably with starting a business, tends to be a mid-life choice for women, with the majority starting up businesses after the age of 35. Self-employed women usually have children at home (kudos to these super-mums), and many go the self-employment route *because* they have family commitments. In most cases, self-employment grants greater schedule flexibility than the rigours of a nine to five job.

The types of businesses that women run reflect the pattern of their occupations in employment. The public administration, education and health fields account for around a quarter of self-employed women, and distribution, hotels and restaurants another fifth.

In financing a new business, women tend to prefer using personal credit cards or remortgaging their home, and men prefer bank loan finance and government and local authority grants.

Being educated about education

A popular myth states that undereducated self-made men dominate the field of entrepreneurship. Anecdotal evidence seems to throw up enough examples of school or university drop-outs to support the theory that education is unnecessary, perhaps even a hindrance, to getting a business started. After all, if Sir Richard Branson (Virgin) could drop out of full time education at 16, and Lord Sugar (Amstrad), Sir Philip Green (BHS and Arcadia, the group that includes Topshop and Miss Selfridge), Sir Bernie Ecclestone (Formula One – Britain's tenth richest man) and Charles Dunstone (Carphone Warehouse) could all give higher education a miss, education can't be that vital.

However, the facts, such as they are, show a rather different picture. Research shows that the more educated the population, the more entrepreneurship takes place. Educated individuals are more likely to identify gaps in the market or understand new technologies. After all, Stelios Haji-Iannou, founder of easyJet, has six degrees to his name, albeit four are honorary. Tony Wheeler, who together with his wife Maureen founded Lonely Planet Publications, has degrees from Warwick University and the London Business School. Jeff Bezos (Amazon) is an alumnus of Princeton and Google's founders, Sergey Brin and Larry Page, graduated from Stanford.

So if you're in education now, stay the course. After all, a key characteristic of successful business starters is persistence and the ability to see things through to completion.

Coming Up with a Winning Idea

Every business starts with the germ of an idea. The idea may stem from nothing more profound than a feeling that customers are getting a raw deal from their present suppliers.

In this section you can find out some tried-and-tested ways to help you come up with a great idea for a new business.

Ranking popular start-up ideas

The government's statistics service produces periodic statistics on the types of businesses operating in the UK.

In terms of the sheer number of business enterprises, the United Kingdom is more a nation of estate agents than of small shopkeepers, as demonstrated in Table 2-1 that shows the types of businesses being operated in Britain in 2010, according to government statistics (http://stats.bis.gov.uk/ed/sme).

Table 2-1 Businesses Operating by Sector, 2010	
Sector	*Total*
Real estate, renting and business activities	1,206,505
Construction	1,009,725
Wholesale and retail trade; repairs	583,280
Other community, social and personal service activities	502,630
Manufacturing	324,330
Transport, storage and communication	294,800
Health and social work	265,585
Agriculture, hunting and forestry; fishing	174,315
Education	168,305
Hotels and restaurants	164,105
Financial intermediation	74,160
Mining and quarrying; electricity, gas and water supply	15,545
All industries	*4,783,285*

You can take one of two views on entering a particularly popular business sector. Either it represents a great idea you're mad to resist, or the business is already awash with competition. In practice, the best view to take is that if others are starting up at least a market opportunity exists. Your task is to research the market thoroughly.

Going with fast growth

Entrepreneur.com produces an annual list of hot business sectors to enter (www.entrepreneur.com/trends). The 2010 list includes:

- ✔ **Buy local:** The buy local ethos has its roots in the farmers' markets movement but the big supermarket chains are getting in on the act, devoting sections of shelf space to local wares.

- ✔ **Discount retailing:** Pound and second-hand businesses are booming on both sides of the Atlantic. The Americans even have a trade association for the sector, the National Association of Resale Professionals.

✔ **Education:** The lack of jobs has sent millions around the globe back to college to train or retrain. Universities in the UK are full to bursting point. Unsurprisingly, a boom is occurring in online learning, tutoring and other private learning facilities.

✔ **Green energy and renewable:** A growing sector because governments the world over are chucking what little money they have at this.

✔ **Senior market:** With the population of over 64s exploding, this is a no-brainer sector to serve. Academics, always quick to latch on to opportunities, have singled out *gerontology* (the study of social, psychological and biological aspects of aging with the view of extending active life whilst enhancing its quality) as one of the hottest areas, with a university scheduled to debut a new master's degree in aging-services management to meet the growing interest in the field.

You can use this information to help pick a fast-growing business area to start your business in. Beginning with the current flowing strongly in the direction you want to travel makes things easier from the start.

Spotting a gap in the market

The classic way to identify a great opportunity is to see something that people would buy if only they knew about it. The demand is latent, lying beneath the surface, waiting for someone – you, hopefully – to recognise that the market is crying out for something no one is yet supplying.

These are some of the ways to go about identifying a market gap:

✔ **Adapting:** Can you take an idea that's already working in another part of the country or abroad and bring it to your own market?

✔ **Locating:** Do customers have to travel too far to reach their present source of supply? This is a classic route to market for shops, hairdressers and other retail-based businesses, including those that can benefit from online fulfilment.

> ✔ **Size:** If you made things a different size, would that appeal to a new market? Anita Roddick of The Body Shop found that she could only buy the beauty products she wanted in huge quantities. By breaking down the quantities and sizes of those products and selling them, she unleashed a huge new demand.
>
> ✔ **Timing:** Are customers happy with current opening hours? If you opened later, earlier or longer, would you tap into a new market?

Revamping an old idea

A good starting point is to look for products or services that used to work really well, but have stopped selling. Ask yourself why they seem to have died out and then try to establish whether, and how, that problem can be overcome. Or you can search overseas or in other markets for products and services that have worked well for years in their home markets but have so far failed to penetrate into your area.

Sometimes with little more than a slight adjustment you can give an old idea a whole new lease of life. For example, the Monopoly game, with its emphasis on the universal appeal of London street names, has been launched in France with Parisian *rues* and in Cornwall using towns rather than streets.

Using the Internet

Many of the first generation of Internet start-ups had nothing unique about their offer, the mere fact that the business was 'on the net' was thought to be enough. Hardly surprisingly, most of them went belly-up in no time at all.

All the basic rules of business apply to Internet businesses. You need a competitive edge – something better and different about your product or service that makes you stand out from the crowd.

However, you also need something about the way you use the Internet to add extra value over and above the traditional ways in which your product or service is sold. Online employment agencies, for example, can add value to their websites by offering clients and applicants useful information such as interview tips, prevailing wage rates and employment law updates.

But using the Internet to take an old idea and turn it into a new and more cost-efficient business can be a winner. Chapter 13 is devoted exclusively to the subject of making a success of getting online and making money.

Solving customer problems

Sometimes existing suppliers just aren't meeting customers' needs. Big firms very often don't have the time to pay attention to all their customers properly because doing so just isn't economic. Recognising that enough people exist with needs and expectations that aren't being met can constitute an opportunity for a new small firm to start up.

Start by recalling the occasions when you've had reason to complain about a product or service. You can extend that by canvassing the experiences of friends, relatives and colleagues. If you spot a recurring complaint, that may be a valuable clue about a problem just waiting to be solved.

Next you can go back over the times when firms you've tried to deal with have put restrictions or barriers in the way of your purchase. If those restrictions seem easy to overcome, and others share your experience, then you may well be on the trail of a new business idea.

Creating inventions and innovations

Inventions and innovations are all too often almost the opposite of either identifying a gap in the market or solving an unsolved problem. Inventors usually start by looking through the other end of the telescope. They find an interesting problem and solve it. There may or may not be a great need for whatever it is they invent.

The Post-it note is a good example of inventors going out on a limb to satisfy themselves rather than to meet a particular need or even solve a burning problem. The story goes that scientists at 3M, a giant American company, came across an adhesive that failed most of their tests. It had poor adhesion qualities because it could be separated from anything it was stuck to. No obvious market existed, but they persevered and pushed the product on their marketing department, saying that the new product had unique properties in that it stuck 'permanently, but temporarily'. The rest, as they say, is history.

Never go down the lonely inventor's route without getting all the help and advice you can get. Chapter 7 gives you details of organisations that can smooth your path from the bench to the market. You should also make sure that someone else hasn't already grabbed your innovation, and that you can put a legal fence around it to keep rustlers out. I deal with copyrights, patents and the like in Chapter 5.

Marketing other people's ideas

You may not have a business idea of your own, but nevertheless feel strongly that you want to work for yourself. This approach isn't unusual. Sometimes an event such as redundancy, early retirement or a financial windfall prompts you to searching for a business idea.

Business ideas very often come from the knowledge and experience gained in previous jobs, but take time to come into focus. Usually, you need a good flow of ideas before one arrives that appeals to you and appears viable.

You can trawl for ideas and opportunities in any number of ways:

✔ **Browse websites.** The Internet is a great source of business ideas. Try Entrepreneurs.com (www.entrepreneur. com/bizoppzone), which lists hundreds of ideas for new businesses, together with information on start-up costs and suggestions for further research. It also has a series of checklists to help you evaluate a business opportunity to see whether it's right for you. Home Working (www.home-workinguk.com) lists dozens of current business ideas exclusively aimed at the British market.

> ✔ **Read business magazines.** Periodicals such as *Start Your Business* magazine (www.sybmagazine.com) present the bones of a number of ideas each month.

> ✔ **Scan papers and periodicals.** Almost all papers and many general magazines too have sections on opportunities and ideas for small businesses.

When answering advertisements for other people's business ideas, do take precautions to ensure that you aren't about to become a victim of a fraudulent venture.

The ASA (www.asa.org.uk) publishes a quarterly list of complaints that it's considered or is investigating. Also check out websites such as www.scambusters.org, www.scam.com and www.fraudguides.com, which track the latest wheezes doing the rounds both on- and offline.

Being better or different

To have any realistic hope of success, every business opportunity must pass one crucial test: the idea or the way the business is to operate must be either different from or better than any other business in the same line of work. In other words you need a *unique selling proposition* (USP), or its Internet equivalent, a *killer application*.

The thinking behind these two propositions is that your business should have a near unbeatable competitive advantage if your product or service offers something highly desirable that others in the field can't easily copy: something that only you can offer. Dyson's initial USP was the bagless cleaner, and Amazon's was 'one-click' shopping, a system for retaining customer details that made buying online a less painful experience.

Inventors need to be persistent. James Dyson took five years and 5,127 prototypes to produce the world's first bagless vacuum cleaner. The result was so successful that, despite patent protection, Hoover tried to imitate the product. Dyson then had an 18-month legal battle on his hands before he finally won a victory against Hoover for patent infringement.

The trick with USPs and killer applications doesn't just lie with developing the idea in the first place, but making it difficult for others to copy it. (Chapter 5 suggests ways to protect your USP.)

If neither you nor the product or service you're offering stands out in some way, then why on earth would anyone want to buy from you? But don't run off with the idea that only new inventions have any hope of success. Often just doing what you say you'll do, when you say you'll do it, is enough to make you stand out from the crowd.

That was all Tom Farmer did when he founded Kwik-Fit. He put his finger on the main criticisms people had of garages. The experience of getting an exhaust fitted or tyres changed was made seriously unpleasant simply because you couldn't rely on the garage's cost estimate or be sure when your car would be ready. The message always was, ring us at 4 p.m. and we'll let you know.

Farmer's big idea was simply to make promises he could keep, to meet deadlines and to keep to estimated costs. And wow, that was enough to build a business that the Ford Motor Company thought was worth the billion pounds it paid for it.

Avoiding obvious mistakes

Your enthusiasm for starting a business is a valuable asset as long as you don't let it blind you to some practical realities. The following list contains some reasoning to resist.

- **Starting in a business sector of which you have little or no previous knowledge or experience.** The grass always looks greener, making business opportunities in distant lands or in technologies with which you have only a passing acquaintance seem disproportionately attractive. Taking this route leads to disaster. Success in business depends on superior market knowledge from the outset and sustaining that knowledge in the face of relentless competition.

- **Putting in more money than you can afford to lose, especially if you have to pay up front.** You need time to learn how business works. If you've spent all your capital and exhausted your capacity for credit on the first spin of the wheel, then you're more a gambler than an entrepreneur. The true entrepreneur takes only a calculated risk. Freddie Laker, who started the first low-cost no-frills airline, bet everything he could raise on buying more planes than he could afford. To compound the risk he bet against the exchange rate between the pound and the dollar, and lost. Learn from Mr Laker's mistake.

✔ **Pitting yourself against established businesses before you're strong enough to resist them.** Laker also broke the third taboo: he took on the big boys on their own ground. He upset the British and American national carriers on their most lucrative routes. There was no way that big, entrenched businesses with deep pockets would yield territory to a newcomer without a fight to the death. That's not to say that Laker's business model was wrong. After all, Ryanair and easyJet have proved that it can work. But those businesses tackled the short-haul market to and from new airfields and, in the case of easyJet, at least started out with tens of millions of pounds of family money that came from a lifetime in the transportation business.

Preparing to Recognise Success

To be truly successful in running your own business you have to both make money and have fun. That's your pay-off for the long hours, the pressure of meeting tough deadlines and the constant stream of problems that accompany most start-up ventures.

One measure of success for any business is just staying in business. That's not as trite a goal as it sounds, nor is it easily achieved, as you can see by looking at the number of businesses that fail each year.

However, survival isn't enough. Cash flow, which I talk about in Chapter 8, is the key to survival, but becoming profitable and making worthwhile use of the assets you employ determine whether staying in business is really worth all your hard work.

Measuring business success

No one in their right mind sets out to run an unsuccessful business, although that's exactly what millions of business founders end up doing. Answering the following questions can act as a check on your progress and keep you on track to success.

- ✔ **Are you meeting your goals and objectives?** In Chapter 6 I talk about setting down business goals. Achieving those goals and objectives is both motivational and, ultimately, the reason you're in business.

- ✔ **Are you making enough money?** This sounds like a daft question, but it may well be the most important one you ask. The answer comes out of your reply to two subsidiary questions:

    - **Can you do better by investing your time and money elsewhere?** If the answer to this question is yes, then go back to the drawing board with your business idea.

    - **Can you make enough money to invest in growing your business?** The answer to this question only becomes clear when you work out your profit, a subject I cover in Chapter 12. But the fact that many businesses don't make enough money to reinvest in themselves is pretty evident when you see scruffy, run-down premises, worn-out equipment and the like.

- ✔ **Can you work to your values?** Anita Roddick's Body Shop had a clearly articulated set of values that she and every employee bought into. Every aspect of the business from product and market development down to the recruitment process promoted this value system – if you weren't green you didn't join. Ms Roddick's philosophy may have been a little higher than you feel like going, but values can help guide you and your team when the going gets tough.

Chapter 3

Can You Do the Business?

....

In This Chapter

▶ Understanding whether being your own boss is right for you

▶ Checking out various ventures

▶ Setting up your business at home

▶ Figuring out your profit motive

▶ Taking a skills inventory to identify any gaps

....

Governments are keen to foster entrepreneurship: new businesses create jobs for individuals and increased prosperity for nations, which are both primary goals for any government. If those new firms don't throw people out of work when recessions start to bite, supporting them becomes doubly attractive.

But people, you included, don't start businesses or grow existing ones simply to please politicians or to give their neighbours employment. They have many reasons for considering self-employment. The idea of escaping the daily grind of working for someone else and being in charge of their own destiny attracts most people. But despite the many potential benefits, they face real challenges and problems, and self-employment isn't a realistic option for everyone.

The questions you need to ask yourself are: Can I do it? Am I really the entrepreneurial type? What are my motivations and aims? How do I find the right business for me? This chapter can help you discover the answers.

Deciding What You Want From a Business

These central themes connecting most reasons for starting up a business: gaining personal satisfaction – making work as much fun as any other aspect of life – and creating wealth – essential if an enterprise is going to last any length of time.

Even when your personality fits and your goals are realistic, you have to make sure that the business you're starting is a good fit for your abilities.

The following sections explore these reasons in more detail.

Gaining personal satisfaction (or, entrepreneurs just wanna have fun)

No one particularly enjoys being told what to do and where and when to do it. Working for someone else's organisation brings all those disadvantages. When you work for yourself, the only person to blame if your job is boring, repetitive or takes up time that you should perhaps spend with family and friends is yourself.

Another source of personal satisfaction comes from the ability to 'do things my way'. Employees are constantly puzzled and often irritated by the decisions their bosses impose on them. All too often managers in big firms say that they'd never spend their own money in the way the powers that be encourage or instruct them to do. Managers and subordinates alike feel constrained by company policy, which seems to set out arbitrary standards for dealing with customers and employees in the same way.

Making money

Apart from winning the lottery, starting your own business is the only possible way to achieve full financial independence. But it isn't risk free. In truth, most people who work for themselves don't become mega rich. However, many do and many more become far wealthier than they would probably have become working for someone else.

You can also earn money working at your own pace when you want to and even help your family to make some money too.

Running your own business means taking more risks than you do if you're working for someone else. If the business fails, you stand to lose far more than your job. If, like most owner managers, you opt for *sole trader status* – someone working usually on his own without forming a limited company (find more on business categories in Chapter 5) – you can end up personally liable for any business debts you incur. This can mean having to sell your home and other assets to meet your obligations. In these circumstances, not only will all your hard work have been to no avail, but you can end up worse off than when you started. Also, winding up a business is far from fun or personally satisfying.

I don't want to discourage you, just to apply a reality check. The truth is that running your own business is hard work that often doesn't pay well at first. You have to be okay with those facts in order to have a chance of success.

Saving the planet

Not everyone has making money as their sole aim when setting up in business. According to the government's figures, around 20,000 'social entrepreneurs' run businesses aiming to achieve sustainable social change and trade with a social or environmental purpose. They contribute almost £25 billion to the national economy and assist local communities by creating jobs, providing ethical products and services using sustainable resources and reinvesting a share of the profits back into society.

Ethical businesses have some unique advantages. For example, according to those running such firms they can relatively easily attract and retain intelligent people. Over 70 per cent of students say that a potential employer's track record is an important factor in job choice. Customers also like ethical firms. According to a recent European Union survey on sustainable consumption, 86 per cent of those polled in the

United Kingdom, Spain, Germany, Greece and Italy said that
they felt very strongly about wanting things to be produced
and marketed responsibly. They also blamed brands for not
providing more environmentally and socially friendly products.

If you want to explore the prospects for starting a social
enterprise, contact the School for Social Entrepreneurs (website: www.sse.org.uk; tel: 020 8981 0300), which can help
with specific and tailored support. If you need funds to start a
social enterprise, contact Bridges Community Ventures (website: www.bridgesventures.com; tel: 020 7262 5566), a venture capital firm with a social mission. Its founding principle
is that all the funds it invests go to businesses with a clear
social purpose as well as aiming to achieve financial returns
for investors.

Exploring Different Types of Business

At one level all businesses are the same – they sell something
to people who want to buy from them, while trying to make an
honest buck along the way. At another level many very different types of business and ways of doing business exist, even
within what superficially can appear to be very similar fields.

Selling to other businesses

Business-to-business (B2B) enterprises, such as those selling
market research, database management, corporate clothing,
management consultancy, telemarketing or graphic design,
involve one businessperson selling to another. The attractions
are that you're dealing with other people who have a definite
need and usually buy in relative large quantities and at regular
intervals. For example, an individual may buy envelopes in
packs of a dozen a few times a year, but a business buys scores,
perhaps even thousands, and puts in an order every month.
Corporate customers are harder to win, but are often worth
more when you have them. And unlike private individuals, businesses like to forge relationships that endure over time.

Some downsides exist too. Business customers expect credit,
perhaps taking between 60 and 90 days to pay up. If they go

bust they may owe a lot of money and take some of their suppliers down with them. You may have to attend exhibitions to make your presence known, a costly and time-consuming process, or advertise in trade directories. Check out these websites to find out more about these topics: www.ideal businessshow.co.uk and www.b2bindex.co.uk.

Opening all hours

Conventional shops, restaurants and the like have long opening hours and have to meet the expectations of increasingly savvy consumers, whose access to the Internet has made them aware of competitive prices as well as high specifications and standards of service. The upside of any form of retailing is that you're almost invariably paid up front. But just because you get the cash in your hand doesn't mean that you don't have to meet exacting standards. Customers are protected in their dealings in a myriad of ways and if you fall short of their legal entitlement you can end up with a bigger bill than a simple cash refund. (I cover legal issues in Chapter 9, 'Marketing Your Wares'.) In conventional retailing you also have to rent premises and stock them with products, both factors that can add significantly to the business risk.

Increasingly, new retail business start-ups are Internet based. The website is in effect the shop window and the stock of products being sold may even be in a warehouse owned by a third party. This keeps up-front costs down but means keeping abreast of fast-changing technologies – the Internet, servers and computer hardware and software. (I look at these in more depth in Chapter 13.)

Making products

One of the attractions of manufacturing is that you have a greater degree of control over the quality, cost and specification of the end product than a retailer or wholesaler might. But with those advantages come some hefty penalties. Factories, equipment, stocks of raw materials and employees are costly overheads. You have to incur these expenses well before you're certain of any orders – an unlikely way into business for someone without previous manufacturing experience and a deep wallet. Such owners also bear some significant risks towards their employees. The UK manufacturing sector reports over 32,000 work-related accidents to the Health and Safety Executive each year. This figure includes over 6,200 major injuries such as fractures and amputations as well as around 40 fatalities.

A more likely route to manufacturing for a new business is subcontracting, where you're working for a manufacturer on part of a product. The most common examples of subcontractors are plumbers, electricians and carpenters in building work, metal and plastic casing production and the like in civil engineering and a wide range of activities in the information technology sector.

Working from Home

Few dedicated statistics exist on the number of people operating home-based enterprises as distinct from those setting up in dedicated premises. IDC, a US-based research firm, claims that around 18 million of the 29 million owner-managed businesses in US are home based. US census data shows that 17.6 million businesses employ no one but the boss. Put these two facts together and working on the reasonable assumption that the majority of home-based businesses are one-man (and one-woman) bands, then around two thirds of all small business would appear to be home based.

Starting a business from home gives you a number of distinct advantages over those plumping for premises straight away. A study by the US Small Business Administration tracking the survival rates on new businesses (www.sba.gov/ADVO/research/business.html >Redefining Business Success) concluded that starting from home significantly improved a founder's chances of succeeding. Other studies coming from organisations less impartial suggest that home-based business are two thirds more likely to survive the crucial first four years of trading and so establish a firm footing.

Finding the space

As a first step list all the activities involved in getting your business to the point where it has something to sell. If you're going to run a bookkeeping service this could be quite a short list. You need a computer, some software and perhaps a leaflet setting out your prices and the range of services on offer. But if you're going to repair musical instruments, say, then you may need much more space including perhaps a workshop.

Clearly, if you live in a cul-de-sac at the end of a narrow lane surrounded by other houses you're unlikely to be allowed to manufacture using hazardous chemicals and have articulated vehicles delivering and collecting in the middle of the night. You also have to consider how your neighbours will be affected, even if you're legally allowed to operate your business.

 You don't, of course, have to carry out every activity related to your business yourself, nor do you have to do it all on your premises. If you think about it you'll see that no business does everything itself.

When you know how much space you need for business and what you'll be doing in that space you can start to scour your home and garden for space to convert to business use. The following sections outline some areas to consider – not an exhaustive list, but enough ideas to kick-start your thinking.

Using the garage

The most obvious discreet space that's separate from the house and likely to be free of family traffic is your garage (if you have one). You can move cars onto the drive or a neighbouring street, subject to your insurance company being happy with that arrangement. According to the RAC Foundation, although 71 per cent of motorists have a garage, only 41 per cent use it to park their car. Most people use it as storage for junk or are too lazy to open the garage doors.

The Garage Conversion Company has sample plans and information on any possible restrictions that may apply (www.garageconversion.com; go to Conversion Ideas and then Home Office).

Parking in the parking space

This area and any private drive could be used for a caravan-based office, although you need to keep in mind that visitors, suppliers and of course you and your family still need to get access to your home.

If you do think that a caravan is worth considering check out that your house deeds allow you because covenants were introduced into the title deeds of new properties from the 1960s onwards to prevent people keeping caravans at home. Even if you're legally allowed to keep a caravan at home you should consider any possible impact on your neighbours and discuss your plans with them. Caravans that could be used as a home office, though probably not as touring caravans, sell for upwards of £1,000.

Planting yourself in the garden

You can install a shed up to 4 square metres without planning consent under certain circumstances. The exact rules are a little complicated; for example the shed can't be bigger than 50 per cent of your garden, you can't erect one in a conservation area and your title deeds can't expressly prohibit you. Great Little Garden (www.greatlittlegarden.co.uk) and Leisure Buildings (www.leisurebuildings.com) both offer advice on planning issues and have sections on using garden sheds as home offices. Sheds that you could use for home office purposes sell at garden centres for £800 upwards.

A further alternative, if space allows, is to rent or buy a portable 'room'. Portakabin (www.portacabin.co.uk) and Foremans Relocatable Building Systems (www.foremans buildings.co.uk) have selections of new and second-hand cabins for rent and sale.

Climbing into an attic

Converting an attic to usable space is likely to be an expensive option and something to consider later after your business is up and running: £10,000 is the entry level price including a ladder and a window; double that if you want to include a WC, plastered walls and a power supply.

You may not need planning permission but as with garden sheds the rules are complicated. Econoloft (www.econoloft.co.uk; go to FAQ and Will I Need Planning) and UK Loft Conversion (www.uk-loft-conversion.com; go to FAQ and Do I Need to Get Building Regulations and Planning Approval?) have information on the rules and much else besides.

Doubling up in the spare room

If you do have a spare or under-utilised room then your search for office space is probably over. It will have heat, light and power and may also be out of the way of general family traffic. If it's currently a bedroom you could get the best of both worlds by putting in a sofa bed and desk with locked drawers. In that way occasional guests can still use the room and you can have it for most of the time. Though far from ideal this can be a low cost option that you can implement quickly.

Options (www.optionsfit.com) provides guides and products for turning your spare room into an office.

Checking out the rules

Whatever business you plan to run from home and whether the space you use is inside or outside of your property you need to check out a number of important rules and regulations before you start up.

Planning consent and building regulations

The extent to which the use of your home and the land it stands on changes determines whether or not you need planning consent or to consider building regulations. You may need permission for any structural alterations, increase in traffic, noise, smells or anything such as operating unreasonable hours or any disturbance that could affect your neighbours.

You can find out informally from your local council before applying and the Communities and Local Government website (www.communities.gov.uk; go to Planning, Building and the Environment) has detailed information on all these matters. You can also get free answers to specific questions using UK Planning's Planning Doctor (www.ukplanning.com), a service supported by some 20 UK councils.

Looking at health, safety and hazards

If you'll be working with materials that are flammable, toxic, give off fumes or are corrosive you should check on the website of the Health and Safety Executive (www.hse.gov.uk/risk) where you'll find detailed guidance and advice on all aspects of safety at work.

Considering insurance

Your home insurance policy won't cover any business activity so you must inform your insurer what you plan to do from home. You can find out more about whether or not what you plan to do from home needs special insurance cover and where to find an insurance company on the Business Link website (www.businesslink.gov.uk; go to Health, Safety, Premises; Insurance; Insure Your Business and Assets – General Insurances; and then Business Insurance If You Work from Home).

Managing the mortgage

Unless you own fully the freehold your property some other party such as a mortgage lender, landlord or freeholder may need to give their permission for you to run a business from home. Even as a freeholder you could find that a covenant has been included into your title deeds to prevent you operating certain activities from your home.

Realising business rates

You currently pay council tax on your home, but after you start using part of it or your grounds for business purposes you could be liable to pay business rates on the part of the property you use for work. You can see some examples of how business rating is applied to home-based businesses on the Valuation Office Agency website (www.voa.gov.uk/council_tax/examples_working_from_home.htm). Some types of small business, particularly those in rural areas providing products or services of particular benefit to the community, are exempt from paying business rates, or pay at a reduced rate. Your local council will have details of such schemes.

Anticipating capital gains tax implications

Any increase in value of your main home is usually free of capital gains tax (CGT) when you sell. However, if you set aside a room or particular area solely for working in then you may be liable for CGT on that proportion of any gain. If you expect to use a large (over 10 per cent) part of your home for business, take professional advice from your accountant and check the HM Revenue and Customs website (www.hmrc.gov.uk/cgt) for more information on CGT and how to calculate any possible liability.

Tax rates and their methods of payment are always in a state of flux, more so since the government introduced emergency measures in 2010 to reduce the country's indebtedness.

Readying for refuse

If your business will create additional or different refuse from that of a normal domestic nature then you should check your local council's policy on collecting for businesses. Also check on NetRegs (www.netregs.gov.uk), the government website that provides free environmental guidance for small businesses in the UK, what your responsibilities are for disposing of waste and hazardous substances.

Keeping in with the neighbours

After you've satisfied yourself that you're complying with all the relevant rules and regulations you'd still be prudent to advise your immediate neighbours of your plans. They may be concerned when they see any unusual comings and goings from your home and a timely word sets their minds at rest. Talking with neighbours will be especially important if you're doing building work.

The Central Office of Information service Directgov has some useful pointers on what might cause problems with neighbours and how to resolve such issues (www.direct.gov.uk; go to Home and Community, Your Neighbourhood Roads and Streets, and then Neighbour Disputes).

Dealing with the family

You might be inclined to slop around just because you're working at home. The dangers here are twofold:

- ✔ You'll give out the wrong signals to everyone around you. As far as they can see you're just 'at home' and as such available for more or less anything that they'd usually expect in a domestic environment.

- ✔ You may not feel as though you're at work yourself. The operative word here is _appropriate_. That doesn't have to mean a suit and tie, but 'smart casual' is a good yardstick and certainly a notch up from what you wear around the house normally, say at weekends.

Dress is a powerful way of sending signals to those around you that you're 'at work'. Here are some other tools to help harmonise business and personal life while you work.

Negotiating with your partner

Your spouse, partner or housemate, whether or not he has a part to play in your business, will be affected and expect to be consulted on how you plan to make use of what he probably sees as his premises. The effect is double if he's picking up the financial slack until your business gets going. These measures help keep them your loved one onside:

- Tell him about your business ideas early on and why you think you'll succeed without disrupting home life unreasonably.

- Discuss the space you need, why you need it and if necessary 'trade' space. If you have to have one of the bedrooms, see what can you offer as compensation. In one rather dramatic case a boat builder needed all of the downstairs rooms for 12 months to build a prototype. The boat builder agreed to build a patio and conservatory the year his first boat sold.

- See whether you can provide a 'quick win' for everyone in your home. For example, if you need broadband Internet offer access to everyone either by setting time aside on your computer or by providing another wireless enabled computer. Or if you're painting and redecorating your office, get other rooms done too.

- Explain the upside potential of what success will mean for everyone in your family when your business gets established: more money; part-time employment for those who want it; and eventually perhaps, a move to business premises.

Assessing Yourself

Business isn't just about ideas and market opportunities. Business is about people too, and at the outset it's mostly about *you*. You need to make sure that you have the temperament to run your own business and the expertise and understanding required for the type of business you have in mind.

The test at the end of this section requires no revision or preparation. You may find out the truth about yourself and whether or not running a business is a great career option or a potential disaster for you.

Discovering your entrepreneurial attributes

Business founders are frequently characterised as people who are bursting with new ideas, highly enthusiastic, hyperactive and insatiably curious. But the more you try to create a clear picture of the typical small business founder, the fuzzier that picture becomes. In reality, the most reliable indicator that a person is likely to start a business is that he has a parent or sibling who runs a business – such people are highly likely to start businesses themselves.

That being said, commentators generally accept some fairly broad characteristics as desirable, if not mandatory. Check whether you recognise yourself in the following list of entrepreneurial traits.

- **Accepting of uncertainty:** An essential characteristic of someone starting a business is a willingness to make decisions and to take risks. This doesn't mean gambling on hunches. It means carefully calculating the odds and deciding which risks to take and when to take them.

  Managers in big business tend to seek to minimise risk by delaying decisions until they know every possible fact. They feel that working without all the facts isn't prudent or desirable. Entrepreneurs, on the other hand, know that by the time the fog of uncertainty has completely lifted, too many people are able to spot the opportunity clearly. In fact, an entrepreneur is usually only interested in decisions that involve accepting a degree of uncertainty.

- **Driven to succeed:** Business founders need to be results oriented. Successful people set themselves goals and get pleasure out of trying to achieve them as quickly as possible and then move on to the next goal. This restlessness is very characteristic.

✔ **Hardworking:** Don't confuse hard work with long hours. At times an owner-manager has to put in 18-hour days, but that shouldn't be the norm. Even if you do work long hours, as long as you enjoy them, that's fine. Enthusiasts can be very productive. Workaholics, on the other hand, have a negative, addictive, driven quality where outputs (results) are less important than inputs. This type of hard work is counterproductive. Real hard work means sticking at a task, however difficult, until you complete it. It means hitting deadlines even when you're dead-beat. It means doing some things you don't much enjoy so you can work your way through to the activities that you enjoy most.

✔ **Healthy:** Apart from being able to put in long days, successful small business owners need to be on the spot to manage the firm every day. Owners are the essential lubricant that keeps the wheels of small business turning. They have to plug any gaps when other people are ill or because they can't afford to employ anyone else for that particular job. They can't afford the luxury of sick leave. Even a week or so's holiday is something of a luxury in the early years of a business's life.

✔ **Innovative:** Most people recognise innovation as the most distinctive trait of business founders. They tend to tackle the unknown; they do things in new and difficult ways; they weave old ideas into new patterns. But they go beyond innovation itself and carry their concept to market rather than remain in an ivory tower.

✔ **Self-disciplined:** Owner-managers need strong personal discipline to keep themselves and the business on the schedule the plan calls for. This is the drumbeat that sets the timing for everything in the company. Get that wrong and you send incorrect signals to every part of the business, both inside and out.

One of the most common pitfalls for novice business-people is failing to recognise the difference between cash and profit. Cash can make people feel wealthy and if it results in a relaxed attitude to corporate status symbols such as cars and luxury office fittings, then failure is just around the corner.

✔ **Totally committed:** You must have complete faith in your business idea. That's the only way in which you can convince all the doubters you're bound to meet along the route. But blind faith isn't enough. You have to back your commitment up with a sound business strategy.

✔ **Well rounded:** Small business founders are rarely geniuses. Some people in their business nearly always have more competence in one field than they could ever aspire to. But the founders have a wide range of ability and a willingness to turn their hand to anything that has to be done to make the venture succeed. They can usually make the product, market it and count the money, but above all they have the self-confidence that lets them move comfortably through uncharted waters.

Working out a business idea that's right for you

Take some time to do a simple exercise that can help you decide what type of business is a good match with your abilities. Take a sheet of paper and draw up two columns. In the left-hand column, list all your hobbies, interests and skills. In the right-hand column, translate those interests into possible business ideas. Table 3-1 shows an example of such a list.

Table 3-1   Matching a Business Idea to Your Skills

Interest/Skills	*Business Ideas*
Cars	Car dealer; repair garage; home tuning service; valet and cleaning/taxi
Cooking	Restaurant; home catering service; providing produce for home freezers
Gardening	Supplying produce to flower or vegetable shops; running a nursery; running a garden centre; landscape design; running a gardening service
Using a computer	Typing authors' manuscripts from home; typing back-up service for busy local companies; running a secretarial agency; web design; bookkeeping service; selling online

Having done this exercise, balance the possibilities against the criteria that are important to you in starting a business.

Weighting your preferences

After you have an idea of some of the businesses you may want to start, you can rank those businesses according to how closely they match what you want from starting a business. Go through the standards you want your business to meet and assign a weight between 1 and 5 to each, on a range from not important at all to absolutely must have. Next, list your possible business opportunities and measure them against the graded criteria.

Table 3-2 shows a sample ranking for Jane Clark, an imaginary ex-secretary with school-aged children who needs work because her husband has been made redundant and is looking for another job. Jane isn't in a position to raise much capital, and she wants her working hours to coincide her children's school day. She wants to run her own show and she wants to enjoy what she does.

Table 3-2	Weighing Up the Factors
Criteria	*Weighting Factor*
Minimal capital required	5
Possibility to work hours that suit lifestyle	5
No need to learn new skills	4
Minimal paperwork	3
Work satisfaction	2
Opportunity to meet interesting people	1

Because minimal capital was an important criterion for Jane she gave it a weight of 5, whereas meeting interesting people, being less important to her, was only weighted 1. Jane gave each of her three business ideas a rating, in points (out of five) against these criteria. A secretarial agency needed capital to start so she gave it only 1 point. Back-up typing needed hardly any money and she allocated 5 points to it. Her worked-out chart is shown in Table 3-3.

Table 3-3

Scoring Alternatives

Criteria	Weighting Factor	Secretarial Agency		Back-up Typing		Authors' Manuscripts	
		Points	Score	Points	Score	Points	Score
Minimal capital	5 ×	1	5	5	25	4	20
Flexible hours	5 ×	1	5	3	15	5	25
No new skills	4 ×	2	8	5	20	5	20
Work satisfaction	3 ×	4	12	1	3	3	9
Minimal paperwork	2 ×	0	0	4	8	5	10
Meeting people	1 ×	4	4	3	3	4	4
Total score			34		74		88

The weighting factor and the rating point multiplied together give a score for each business idea. The highest score indicates the business that best meets Jane's criteria. In this case, typing authors' manuscripts scored over back-up typing, because Jane could do it exactly when it suited her.

Chapter 4

Testing Feasibility

· ·

· ·

*Y*ou need to decide whether or not starting up your own business is for you. Maybe you've reached a tentative decision on whether to go it alone or to join forces with others who have valuable resources or ideas to add to your own, and now have the bones of an idea of what type of business you want to start, buy into, franchise or enter in some other way.

So all you have to do now is wait for the customers to turn up and the cash to roll in. Right? Wrong, regrettably. Although you're beyond square one, you have a good few miles to cover before you can be confident that your big business idea is actually going to work and make money. This chapter gives you the right questions to ask to make you as sure as you can be that you have the best shot at success.

Finding Enough Product or People

The first test of feasibility is whether you can get enough goods to sell or enough people to provide the service you're offering. You need to be sure that you can get your product manufactured at the rate and quantity to meet your needs. Likewise, if you're starting a service business, you need to be sure that you can hire people with the skills you need, whether they're housecleaners or web page designers.

Of course, if you're buying into a franchise or joining an existing business or co-operative, these issues are already addressed for the most part. Still, it never hurts to do your own assessment of the *supply chain* linking you to your source of materials and onwards to your end customers, if only to familiarise yourself with the process.

How much is enough?

The amount of goods or services you need depends in part on the scale of your ambitions and also on what you believe the market can bear. If the area in which you plan to open a restaurant has a total population of 100 people within a 50-mile radius, that fact alone limits the scale of your venture.

It makes sense to work backwards to answer this question. For example, if you want to make at least as much money from your business as you have in wages from your current job, then you can use that figure to work out the initial scale of your level of output. As a rough rule of thumb, if you want to make £10,000 profit before tax, a business involved in manufacturing or processing materials needs to generate between £80,000 and £100,000 worth of orders. Taking away your anticipated profit from the sales target leaves you with the value of the goods and services you need to buy in.

Buying in equipment and supplies

There are four main areas to check out:

- ✔ **Consumable materials:** If you're making things yourself, you need to check out suppliers of raw materials. Even if, like mail-order firms, you're buying in finished product, you should check that out too. You can search on Google, Yahoo!, Bing, Ask Jeeves or any of the major search engines for almost any product or service. However, unless the quantities are large and significantly better terms can be had elsewhere, you're better sticking to local suppliers for consumables. This is an inexpensive way to build up goodwill in the local community and may even create business for you. See *Kellysearch* and

Kompass directories for details of suppliers of consumables (see the next bullet for details).

✔ **Equipment:** If you're going to make any or all of your products yourself, you need to check out suppliers, delivery times, payment terms and so forth for the equipment you need for the production processes. You first need to check out the output levels and quality standards of any equipment you want, to make sure it meets your needs. You can find equipment suppliers in either *Kellysearch* (www.kellysearch.co.uk) or *Kompass* (www.kompass.com). These two directories between them contain information on 23 million products and services from 2.7 million suppliers in over 70 countries. These directories are available both in your local business library and, to a limited extent, online.

✔ **Finished goods:** It's usually a better use of scarce cash for a new business to buy in product that's as close to its finished state as possible, leaving you only the high-value-added tasks to complete. Few niche mail-order catalogue businesses make any of their own product; their key skills lie in merchandise selection, advertising copy, web design or buying in the right mailing lists. *Kellysearch* and *Kompass* directories list almost every finished goods supplier.

✔ **Premises:** Finding the right premises can be the limiting factor for some businesses. If, for example, you need to be in a particular type of area, as with restaurants, coffee shops and night clubs, it could take months for the right place to come on the market and even longer to get planning or change-of-use consent if you require that. When you have a clear idea of the type of premises you want, check out all the commercial estate agents in the area. It makes sense to have a few alternative locations in your plans too.

Hiring in help

Unless you plan to do everything yourself on day one, you need to confirm that people with the skills you need are available in your area at wage rates you can afford. Start by looking in the situations vacant section of your local newspaper under the appropriate headings. If you need kitchen staff for your new restaurant and the paper has 20 pages of advertisers desperately looking for staff, then you may well have a problem on your hands. Chapter 10 looks at finding employees for your business.

Sizing Up the Market

You need to ensure that enough customers, with sufficient money to spend, exist to create a viable marketplace for your products or services. You must also see who's competing against you for their business. In other words, you need to research your market.

Market research is something that potential financial backers – be they banks or other institutions – insist on. And in this they're doing you a favour. Many businesses started with private money fail because the founders don't thoroughly research the market at the outset.

Whatever your business idea, you must undertake some well-thought-out market research before you invest any money or approach anyone else to invest in your venture.

Market research has three main purposes:

- ✔ **To build credibility for your business idea:** You must prove, first to your own satisfaction and later to outside financiers, that you thoroughly understand the marketplace for your product or service. This proof is vital to attracting resources to build the new venture.

- ✔ **To develop a realistic market entry strategy:** A successful marketing strategy is based on a clear understanding of genuine customer needs and on the assurance that product quality, price and promotional and distribution methods are mutually supportive and clearly focused on target customers.

- ✔ **To gain understanding of the total market, both customers and competition:** You need sufficient information on your potential customers, competitors and market to ensure that your market strategy is at least on the target, if not on the bull's-eye itself. If you miss the target altogether, which you may well do without research, you may not have the necessary cash resources for a second shot.

The military motto 'Time spent in reconnaissance is rarely time wasted' holds true for business as well.

The following sections cover the areas you need to consider to make sure you've properly sized up your business sector.

Figuring out what you need to know

Before embarking on your market research, set clear and precise objectives. You don't want just to find out interesting information about the market in general, and you don't want to spend time and money exploring the whole market when your target is merely a segment of that market. (I talk about segmenting the market in the 'Finding your segment of the market' section coming up in a bit.)

You have to figure out who your target customer is and what you need to know about him or her. For example, if you're planning to open a shop selling to young, fashion-conscious women, your research objective may be to find out how many women between the ages of 18 and 28, who make at least £25,000 per annum, live or work within two miles of your chosen shop position. That gives you some idea of whether the market can support a venture such as yours.

You also want to know what the existing market is for your product and how much money your potential customers spend on similar products. You can get a measure of such spending from Mintel reports (www.mintel.com). Mintel publishes over 400 reports every year covering key sectors such as fast-moving consumer goods (FMCG), financial services, media, retail, leisure and education. Worldwide office locations include London, Chicago, New York, Shanghai, Tokyo and Sydney.

You also want to know as much as you can about your competitors – their share of the market, their marketing strategy, their customer profile, product pricing schemes and so on.

You need to research in particular:

> ✔ **Your customers:** Who's going to buy your goods and services? What particular customer needs does your business meet? How many of them are there, are their

numbers growing or contracting, how much do they spend and how often do they buy?

✓ **Your competitors:** Which established businesses are already meeting the needs of your potential customers? What are their strengths and weaknesses? Are they currently failing their customers in some way that you can improve on?

✓ **Your product or service:** Can, or should, it be tailored to meet the needs of particular groups of customers? For example, if you're starting up a delivery business, professional clients may require a same-day service, but members of the public at large may be happy to get goods in a day or two, provided this is less costly.

✓ **The price you should charge:** All too often small firms confine their research on pricing to seeing what the competition charges and either matching it or beating it. That may be a way to get business, but it's not the best route to profitable business. You need to know what price is perceived as being too cheap, what represents good value for money and what's seen as a rip-off, so you can pitch in at the right price for your offering.

✓ **Which promotional material will reach your customers:** What newspapers and journals do they read and which of these is most likely to influence their buying decision?

✓ **Your location:** From where can you reach your customers most easily and at minimum cost?

✓ **Most effective sales method:** Can you use telesales, the Internet or a catalogue, or do customers only buy face to face either from a salesperson or from a retail outlet?

Research isn't just essential in starting a business but should become an integral part in the ongoing life of the business.

Budgeting for your research

Market research isn't free even if you do it yourself. At the very least, you have to consider your time. You may also spend money on journals, phone calls, letters and field visits. And if you employ a professional market research firm, your budgeting needs shoot to the top of the scale.

For example, a survey of 200 executives responsible for office equipment purchasing decisions cost one company £12,000. In-depth interviews with 20 banking consumers cost £8,000.

Doing the research in-house may save costs but limit the objectivity of the research. If time is your most valuable commodity, it may make sense to get an outside agency to do the work. Another argument for getting professional research is that it may carry more clout with investors.

Whatever the cost of research, you need to assess its value to you when you're setting your budget. So if getting it wrong will cost £100,000, then £5,000 spent on market research may be a good investment.

Doing the preliminary research

Research methods range from doing it all from your desk to getting out in the field yourself and asking questions – or hiring someone to do it for you. The following sections explore the various methods you can use to find out what you need to know.

Doing research behind your desk

When you know the questions you want answers to, the next step is finding out whether someone else has the answers already. Much of the information you need may well be published, so you can do at least some of your market research in a comfortable chair either in your home or in a good library. Even if you use other research methods, it's well worth doing a little desk research first.

Gathering information at the library

Thousands of libraries in the UK and tens of thousands elsewhere in the world between them contain more desk research data than any entrepreneur ever requires. Libraries offer any number of excellent information sources. You can either take yourself to your local library or bring the library's information to you via the Internet if you're dealing with one of the reference libraries in a larger city or town.

You can find details of every journal, paper and magazine's readership in *BRAD* (British Rate and Data) and every company has to file details of its profits, assets, liabilities and directors at Companies House, the place where all business details and accounts are kept (www.companieshouse.org.uk). Their WebCHeck service offers a free-of-charge, searchable Company Names and Address Index that covers 2 million companies either by name or unique company registration number.Some market information data costs hundreds of pounds and some is available only to subscribers who pay thousands of pounds to have it on tap. Fortunately for you, your library (or an Internet link to a library) may have the relevant directory, publication or research study on its shelves.

Librarians are trained, amongst other skills, to archive and retrieve information and data from their own libraries and increasingly from Internet data sources as well. Thus, they represent an invaluable resource that you should tap into early in the research process. You can benefit many times from their knowledge at no cost, or you may want to make use of the research service some libraries offer to business users at fairly modest rates.

Apart from public libraries, you can access hundreds of university libraries, specialist science and technology libraries, and government collections of data with little difficulty.

Using the power of the Internet

The Internet can be a powerful research tool. However, it has some particular strengths and weaknesses that you need to keep in mind when using it.

Strengths of the Internet include:

- ✔ Offers cheap access and often free information
- ✔ Provides good background information
- ✔ Produces information quickly
- ✔ Covers a wide geographic scope

Weaknesses of the Internet include:

- ✔ The bias is strongly towards the US
- ✔ Coverage of any given subject may be patchy
- ✔ Authority and credentials are often lacking

It would be a brave or foolhardy entrepreneur who started up in business or set out to launch new products or services without at least spending a day or two surfing the Internet. At the very least this lets you know whether anyone else has taken your business idea to market. At best, it may save you lots of legwork around libraries, if the information you want is available online.

These are some of the most useful online sources of information on markets:

- ✔ **Corporate Information** (www.corporateinformation. com; go to Tools and then Research Links) is a business information site covering the main world economies, offering plenty of free information. This link takes you to sources of business information in over 100 countries.

- ✔ **Doing Business** (www.doingbusiness.org): This is the World Bank's database that provides objective measures of business regulations across 183 countries and produces occasional reports on major cities within those countries. You can find out everything from the rules on opening and closing a business to trading across borders, tax rates, employment laws, enforcing contracts and much more. The site also has a tool for comparing countries to rank them by the criteria you consider most important.

- ✔ **Trade Association Forum** (www.taforum.org; go to Directories and then Association Directory) is the online directory of trade associations on whose websites are links to industry-relevant online research sources. For example, you can find the Baby Products Association listed, at whose website you can find details of the 238 companies operating in the sector with their contact details.

- ✔ **Warc** (www.warc.com) claims to provide the most comprehensive marketing information service in the world. Their online guide to world advertising trends is based on latest annual advertising expenditure data across all main media for more than 60 countries, outlining key trends in media investment over the last ten years.

Getting to the grass roots

If the market information you need isn't already available, and the chances are that it isn't, then you need to find the answers yourself.

Going out into the marketplace to do market research is known as *field research*, or sometimes *primary research*, by marketing professionals.

Field research allows you to gather information directly related to your venture and to fine-tune results you get from other sources. For example, entrepreneurs interested in opening a classical music shop in Exeter aimed at young people were encouraged when desk research showed that of a total population of 250,000, 25 per cent were under 30. However, the research didn't tell them what percentage of this 25 per cent was interested in classical music nor how much money each potential customer might spend. Field research showed that 1 per cent was interested in classical music and would spend £2 a week, suggesting a potential market of only £65,000 a year ($250,000 \times 25\% \times 1\% \times £2 \times 52$)! The entrepreneurs sensibly decided to investigate Birmingham and London instead. But at least the cost had been only two damp afternoons spent in Exeter, rather than the horror of having to dispose of a lease on an unsuccessful shop.

Most field research consists of an interviewer putting questions to a respondent either face to face, by post or telephone or online.

Internet surveys using questionnaires similar to those conducted by post or on the telephone are growing in popularity. On the plus side, the other survey methods involve having the data entered or transcribed at your expense, but with an Internet survey the respondent enters the data. Internet survey software also comes with the means of readily analysing the data, turning it into useful tables and charts. Such software may also have a statistical package to check out the validity of the data itself and so give you some idea how much reliance to place on it.

Buying the software to carry out Internet surveys may be expensive, but you can rent it and pay per respondent for each survey you do.

Check out companies such as Free Online Surveys (`http://free-online-surveys.co.uk`) and Zoomerang (`www.zoomerang.com`) that provide software that lets you carry out online surveys and analyse the data quickly. Most of these organisations offer free trials – Free Online Surveys, for example, allows you to create a survey of up to 20 questions and receive up to 50 responses over a ten-day period, beginning when you start creating your survey. An upgrade to their SurveyExtra lets you ask as many questions as you want with up to 1,000 responses for £19.95 per month.

Once upon a time samples of Internet users were heavily biased towards students, big companies and university academics. Not any more. In 2010, according to the Office for National Statistics, 30.1 million adults in the UK (60 per cent) accessed the Internet every day or almost every day. This is nearly double the estimate in 2006 of 16.5 million. This means you can canvas almost everyone's views.

Working Out Whether You Can Make Money

There isn't much point in trying to get a new business off the ground if it's going to take more money than you can raise or take longer to reach break even and turn in a profit than you can possibly survive unaided. I look in more detail at financial matters such as profits and margins in Chapter 12, but you can't start looking at the figures soon enough. Doing some rough figures at the outset can save you a lot of time pursuing unrealistic or unprofitable business opportunities.

Estimating start-up costs

Setting up a business requires money – you can't get away from that. You have rent to pay, materials and equipment to purchase, and all before you receive any income. Starting a business on the road to success involves ensuring that you have sufficient money to survive until the point where income continually exceeds expenditure.

Raising this initial money and the subsequent financial management of the business are therefore vital, and you should take great care over these matters. Unfortunately, more businesses fail due to lack of sufficient day-to-day cash and financial management than for any other reason.

The first big question is to establish how much money you need. Look at every possible cost and divide them into one-off, fixed or variable categories. The *fixed costs* are those that you have to pay even if you make no sales (rent, rates, possibly some staff costs, repayments on any loans and so on) as well as some *one-off costs*, or one-time purchases such as buying a vehicle or computer, which you won't repeat after the business is up and running. *Variable costs* are those that vary depending on the level of your sales (raw materials, production and distribution costs, and so on).

Your finance requirements are shown very clearly on your cash-flow forecast, which is a table showing, usually on a monthly basis, the amount of money actually received into the business, and the amount of money paid out.

According to the Bank of England's report on small business finance, the average start-up cost for a new business in the UK is just over £35,000. However, that average conceals some wide variations. Some start-ups, particularly those in technology or manufacturing, may require hundreds, thousands or even millions of pounds, but others, such as those run from home, may cost very little or nothing.

Forecasting sales

All forecasts may turn out to be wrong, but it's important to demonstrate in your strategy that you've thought through the factors that affect performance. You should also show how you can deliver satisfactory results even when many of these factors work against you. You need this information to give you comfort, and both your backers and employees alike measure the downside risk to evaluate the worst scenario and its likely effects, and look towards an ultimate exit route.

Here are some guidelines to help you make an initial sales forecast:

  ✔ **Credible projections:** Your overall projections have to be believable. Most lenders and investors have extensive experience of similar business proposals. Unlike you, they have the benefit of hindsight, being able to look back several years at other ventures they've backed and see how they fared in practice as compared with their initial forecasts.

You can gather some useful knowledge on similar businesses yourself by researching company records (at Companies House, www.companieshouse.gov.uk, where the accounts of most British companies are kept) or by talking with the founders of similar ventures who aren't your direct competitors.

✔ **Customers:** How many customers and potential customers do you know who are likely to buy from you, and how much might they buy? Here you can use many types of data on which to base reasonable sales projections. You can interview a sample of prospective customers, issue a press release or advertisement to gauge response and exhibit at trade shows to obtain customer reactions. If your product or service needs to be on an approved list before it can be bought, then your business plan should confirm that you have that approval, or less desirably, show how you can get it.

You should also look at seasonal factors that may cause sales to be high or low at certain periods in the year. This is particularly significant for cash-flow projections. You should then relate your seasonal, customer-based forecast to your capacity to make or sell at this rate. Sometimes your inability to recruit or increase capacity may limit your sales forecasts.

✔ **Desired income:** This approach to estimating sales embraces the concept that forecasts may also accommodate the realistic aims of the proprietor. Indeed, you can go further and state that the whole purpose of strategy is to ensure that the business achieves certain forecasts. This is more likely to be the case in a mature company with proven products and markets than in a start-up.

Nevertheless, an element of 'How much do we need to earn?' must play a part in forecasting, if only to signal when a business idea isn't worth pursuing.

One extreme of the desired income approach to forecasting comes from those entrepreneurs who think that the forecasts are the business plan. Such people cover the business plan with a mass of largely unconnected numbers. With reams of computer printout covering every variation possible in business, complete with sensitivity analysis, these people are invariably a big turn-off with financiers.

✔ **Market guidelines:** Some businesses have accepted formulas you can use to estimate sales. This is particularly true in retailing, where location studies, traffic counts and population density are known factors.

✔ **Market share:** How big is the market for your product or service? Is it growing or contracting and at what rate, as a percentage per annum? What is the economic and competitive position? These are all factors that can provide a market share basis for your forecasts. An entry market share of more than a few per cent is most unusual. But beware of turning this argument on its head. Unsubstantiated statements such as 'In a market of £1 billion per annum we can easily capture 1 per cent, which is £1 million a year' impress no investor.

Exceeding break even

So far I've taken certain decisions for granted and ignored how to cost the product or service you're marketing, and indeed, how to set the selling price.

Your goal is to get past break even, the point at which you've covered all your costs, and into the realm of making profits as quickly as possible. So these decisions are clearly important if you want to be sure of making a profit.

At first glance the problem is simple. You just add up all the costs and charge a bit more. The more you charge above your costs, provided the customers keep on buying, the more profit you make. Unfortunately, as soon as you start to do the sums the problem gets a little more complex. For a start, not all costs have the same characteristics. Some costs, for example, don't change however much you sell. If you're running a shop, the rent and rates are relatively constant figures, completely independent of the volume of your sales. On the other hand, the cost of the products sold from the shop is completely dependent on volume. The more you sell, the more it costs you to buy in stock. You can't really add up those two types of costs until you've made an assumption about how much you plan to sell.

Part II
Making and Funding Your Plan

'Look, Filligrew, this company has always insisted its employees leave their private lives at home.'

In this part . . .

Running your own business means constantly juggling resources. You need to focus on a product or service that you can provide better than or differently to those already in the market. This part helps you decide on the best way to develop and communicate your marketing strategy, set a selling price, decide on a place to operate from, and how and where to advertise.

Having customers means you have to produce product or deliver your service, which requires cash that you in turn will have to find. Before any financier will discuss your cash needs seriously you will need to put together your business plan.

Chapter 5

Structuring Your Business

*W*hen you start your business you have to make a decision more or less from the outset on the legal structure you're going to use to trade. Although that's an important decision, luckily, it's not an irrevocable one. You can change structures as your business grows – though not without some cost and paperwork.

The simplest structure is to make all the business decisions yourself and take all the risk personally. You don't have to shoulder all the responsibilities when you start a business, though most people initially do so. It may be great doing everything your way, at last, after the frustrations of working for someone else. But it can be lonely or even scary with no one with whom you can talk over the day-to-day problems and share the responsibility of decision making.

If your business requires substantial investment, or involves other people who'll have a more or less equal hand in the venture alongside you, then your decision about the legal structure of the business is a little more complicated. In this chapter you can find all the important factors to consider when deciding on the legal structure for your business.

Choosing the Right Structure

Different legal frameworks exist for the ownership of a business and not all are equally appropriate for everyone.

Most small businesses in the UK start out as sole proprietorships; however, by the time they register for VAT (value added tax) – in other words, after they're up and running – then owners tend to seek the shelter of limited liability.

One of the many factors you have to consider when deciding on the legal structure of your business is tax, including VAT and its implications.

But even more compelling reasons than tax to choose one structure over another may exist. Not all sources of finance are open to every type of business. When you know how much money you need either to start up or to grow a business and what you need that money for, you're in a better position to make an informed choice about the best way to structure your business. If you need to raise large sums of money from the outset for research and development, for example, then a limited company may be your only realistic option, with its access to risk capital. And if you're nervous about embroiling your finances with other people's, a partnership isn't an attractive option.

In general, the more money you require and the riskier the venture, the more likely it is that a limited company is the appropriate structure.

The good news is that you can change your legal structure at more or less any time. Even if you go the full distance and form a company and get it listed on the stock exchange, you can delist and go private.

Both your accountant and your lawyer can help you with choosing your legal form.

Going into Business by Yourself

You may want to develop your own unique ideas for a product or service, and if so, setting up your own business from the drawing board may be your only option. You may want to start a home-based business that you can run in your own time. You may want to start a business because you want to do things the right way, after working for an employer who goes about things in the wrong way.

Doing things your own way is much easier if you're working alone, rather than, say, buying someone else's business that already has its routines and working practices established.

Advantages

Working for and by yourself has several things going for it:

✔ It may be possible to start the business in your spare time. This allows you to gain more confidence in the future success of your proposed venture before either giving up your job or pumping your life savings into the business.

✔ If you have limited money to invest in your new venture, you may not need to spend it all at the start of the project. This also means that if things do start to go wrong, it's easier to restrict the losses.

✔ Starting a business isn't just about money. Setting up and running a successful business has the potential to give you a feeling of personal achievement, which may not exist to quite the same extent if you buy someone else's business, for example.

Disadvantages

Going it alone isn't all fun and games. Some of the disadvantages are:

✔ Your business will take time to grow. It may not be able to support your current personal financial obligations for many months or years.

✔ A lot of one-off administration is involved in setting up a new business, such as registering for VAT and PAYE (pay as you earn, or income tax), getting business stationery, setting up phone, fax and Internet connections at your trading premises and registering your business name, in addition to actually trading.

These tasks can be very time consuming and frustrating in the short term, and very costly in the long run if you get them wrong. Unfortunately, these tasks are often not easily delegated and can be expensive if you get other people to do them. If you buy a business or take up a franchise, these basic administrative tasks should have already been dealt with.

✔ You have no one to bounce ideas off, or to share responsibility with when things go wrong.

✔ As a result of the perceived riskiness, generally you may have more difficulty borrowing money to fund a start-up than to invest in an established profitable business.

Settling on sole-trader status

The vast majority of new businesses are essentially one-man (or one-woman) bands. As such, they're free to choose the simplest legal structure, known by terms such as *sole trader* or *sole proprietor*. This structure has the merit of being relatively formality free and having few rules about the records you have to keep. As a sole proprietor you don't have to have your accounts audited or file financial information on your business.

If you're a sole trader, no legal distinction exists between you and your business. Your business is one of your personal assets, just as your house or car is. Following from this, if your business should fail your creditors have a right not only to the assets of the business, but also to your personal assets too.

Working with a Limited Number of Other People

Unless you're the self-contained type who prefers going it alone, you have to work alongside other people to get your business going. Not just suppliers or employees or bankers and the like – everyone in business has to do that to a greater or lesser extent.

The upside of going into business with others is that you have someone on your side to talk to when the going gets tough, and it will do from time to time. Two heads are very often better than one. Also, you have the advantage of extra physical and mental resources when they matter most, from the very outset.

However, it's not a one-sided equation, unfortunately. With other people come other points of view, other agendas and the opportunity to disagree, argue and misunderstand.

Taking on an existing business

If you don't have a solid business idea of your own, with a clear vision and strategy, you can consider using someone else's wholly formed business. You can think of such ventures as virtually a business-in-a-box. Just buy it, take it home, open it up and start trading. Of course it's not always quite that easy, but in broad principle that's what network marketing, franchising and co-operative ventures are all about.

Forming a partnership

A *partnership* is effectively a collection of sole traders or proprietors. Very few restrictions apply to setting up in business with another person (or persons) in partnership, and several definite advantages exist:

- ✔ Pooling your resources means you have more capital.
- ✔ You bring several sets of skills to the business, hopefully, instead of just one.
- ✔ If one of you is ill or disabled, the business can still carry on.

Partnerships are a common structure that people who started out on their own use when they want to expand.

The legal regulations governing partnerships in essence assume that competent businesspeople should know what they're doing. The law merely provides a framework of agreement, which applies 'in the absence of agreement to the contrary'.

Looking at limited partnerships

One option that can reduce the more painful consequences of entering a partnership is to have your involvement registered as a limited partnership. A limited partnership works like this: one or more general partners must be involved with the same basic rights and responsibilities (including unlimited liability) as in any general partnership. In addition there can be one or more limited partners who are usually passive investors. The big difference between a general partner and a limited partner is that the limited partner isn't personally liable for debts of the partnership so long as they play no active part in the business. The most a limited partner can lose is the amount that he:

✔ Paid or agreed to pay into the partnership as a capital contribution

✔ Received from the partnership after it became insolvent

The advantage of a limited partnership as a business structure is that it provides a way for business owners to raise money (from the limited partners) without having either to take in new partners who are active in the business, or to form a limited company. Often, a general partnership that's been operating for years creates a limited partnership to finance expansion.

Checking out co-operatives

If making money is much lower on your list of priorities for starting up in business than being involved in the decisions of an ethical enterprise, then joining a co-operative or starting your own is an idea worth exploring.

A *co-operative* is an autonomous association of people united voluntarily to meet their common economic, social and cultural needs and aspirations through a jointly owned and democratically controlled enterprise.

You must have at least seven members at the outset, though they don't all have to be full-time workers at first.

Like a limited company, a registered co-operative has limited liability for its members and must file annual accounts.

Although the most visible co-operatives are the high-street shops and supermarkets, pretty well any type of business can operate as a co-operative.

If you choose to form a co-operative, you can pay from £90 to register with the Chief Registrar of Friendly Societies. Not all co-operatives bother to register because doing so isn't mandatory, but if you don't register, the law regards your co-operative as a partnership with unlimited liability.

 You can find out everything you need to know about the size, structure and prospects of co-operatives in the UK in a free 36-page report that you can download from www.uk.coop/ resources/documents/uk-co-operative-economy-2010.

Finding Your Way to Franchising

Franchising can be a good first step into self-employment for those with business experience but no actual experience of running a business – often the case with those who are looking for something to do following a corporate career.

 Franchising is a marketing technique used to improve and expand the distribution of a product or service. The franchiser supplies the product or teaches the service to you, the franchisee, who in turn sells it to the public. In return for this, you pay a fee and a continuing royalty, based usually on turnover. The franchiser may also require you to buy materials or ingredients from it, which gives it an additional income stream. The advantage to you is a relatively safe and quick way of getting into business for yourself, but with the support and advice of an experienced organisation close at hand.

The franchising company can expand its distribution with minimum strain on its own capital and have the services of a highly motivated team of owner-managers. Franchising isn't a path to great riches, nor is it for the truly independent spirit, because policy and profits still come from on high.

According to the latest annual franchise survey produced by the National Westminster Bank and the British Franchise Association (www.british-franchise.org), in 2010 some 34,800 franchised units operated through 842 franchise chains (McDonald's, Domino's Pizzas, Kall Kwik and the like). The turnover of the industry grew to £11.8 billion, up by 42 per cent over the past decade and twice as fast as the economy as a whole. The number of people employed in franchising, directly and indirectly, is estimated to be 465,000. London and the South East, the South West, North West, West and East Midlands are the main regions for franchising activity. London and the Southeast alone account for 30 per cent of all franchise units.

Network Marketing is a less formal and lower cost option than franchising. Network Marketing can make sense for people who really believe in a particular product and want to sell it but don't have the means to tie up a lot of money buying a franchise or other business, or don't have a great idea of their own. Just remember to check out the network company using trade associations such as the Direct Selling Association (www.dsa.org.uk). You won't get rich in a hurry, or probably ever, but if you take care you probably won't lose your shirt either.

You can meet franchisers and hear their pitch at one of the dozen or so franchise exhibitions held around the country each year. The BFA Diary page (www.thebfa.org/diary. asp) gives details of dates and venues.

Founding a Larger Company

If your business looks like it will need a substantial amount of money from the outset and will be taking on the risk of customers owing money, as with any manufacturing venture, then the legal structures looked at so far may not be right for you.

In this section you can find out about the advantages and disadvantages of going for a limited company, or buying out a company already in business.

Opting for a limited company

As the name suggests, in this form of business your liability is limited to the amount you contribute by way of share capital.

Two shareholders, one of whom must be a director, can form a limited company. You must also appoint a company secretary, who can be a shareholder, director or an outside person such as an accountant or lawyer.

You can buy a company 'off the shelf' from a registration agent, and then adapt it to suit your own purposes. This involves changing the name, shareholders and articles of association and takes a couple of weeks to arrange. Alternatively, you can form your own company.

A limited company has a legal identity of its own, separate from the people who own or run it. This means that, in the event of failure, creditors' claims are restricted to the assets of the company. The shareholders of the business aren't liable as individuals for the business debts beyond the paid-up value of their shares. This applies even if the shareholders are working directors, unless of course the company has been trading fraudulently. In practice, the ability to limit liability is restricted these days as most lenders, including the banks, often insist on personal guarantees from the directors. Other advantages include the freedom to raise capital by selling shares.

Disadvantages include the legal requirement for the company's accounts to be audited and filed for public inspection.

 When a company is first registered it must send to Companies House (www.companieshouse.org.uk), the place where all business details and accounts are kept, a copy of its memorandum and articles of association and Form 10, which contains the address of the company's registered office and details of its directors and company secretary. Companies House organises or attends a variety of seminars and exhibitions to support and advise businesses and to support new directors and secretaries. You can find details of these on the events section of the Companies House website (www.companieshouse.org.uk/about/chEvents.shtml).

Buying out a business

Buying out an existing business is particularly well suited to people who have extensive experience of general business management but lack detailed technical or product knowledge.

When you buy an established business, you not only pay for the basic assets of the business, but also the accumulated time and effort that the previous owner spent growing the business to its present state. You can think of this extra asset as *goodwill*. The better the business, the more the 'goodwill' costs you.

Advantages of buying a business include:

- ✔ You acquire some of the experience and expertise you don't have. It's much easier, and almost invariably less costly, to learn from the mistakes other people have made in the past, rather than making all these mistakes yourself.

- ✔ You gain both access to your potential customers and the credibility of a trading history from the outset, which can save months if not years of hard work in building relationships.

- ✔ If the business you buy is already profitable, you can pay yourself a living wage from the outset.

- ✔ Bank financing may be easier to acquire for an established business than for a riskier start-up business.

Disadvantages of buying a business include:

- ✔ You run the risk of acquiring the existing unsolved problems and mistakes of the person who's selling it.

- ✔ Identifying the right potential acquisition and negotiating a purchase can take a very long time, and there's no guarantee that you'll succeed at your first attempt.

- ✔ The professional fees associated with buying a business can be a significant, though necessary, cost. If you buy a very small business, the total professional fees associated with the transaction are a major percentage of the total cost of your investment, perhaps as much as 15 or 20 per cent. Experienced solicitors and accountants are vital to this process. They're your safeguards to ensure that you know exactly what you're buying.

Contact these organisations to find out more about buying a business and to see listings of businesses for sale:

- ✔ Businesses For Sale (www.businessesforsale.com) has over 55,000 businesses for sale in the UK, as well as listings of firms in Spain, the USA, Australia, Canada, India, Ireland, New Zealand and France.

- ✔ Christie & Co (www.christie.com, tel. 0207 227 0700) claims to have the largest database of businesses for sale in Europe. It's the recognised market leader in the hotel, catering, leisure and retail markets and is also expanding into healthcare.

- ✔ Daltons (www.daltonsbusiness.com) has an online database of over 30,000 businesses for sale around the United Kingdom and some overseas countries.

Looking at Legal Issues in Marketing

Nothing in business escapes the legal eye of the law and marketing is no exception. If anything, marketing is likely to produce more grey areas from a legal point of view than most other aspects. You have patent and copyright issues to consider, for example.

A number of vital aspects of your business distinguish it from other similar firms operating in or near to your area of operations. Having invested time, energy and money in acquiring these distinguishing factors, you need to take steps to preserve any benefits they provide you with. Intellectual property, often known as IP, is the generic title covering the area of law that allows people to own their creativity and innovation in the same way that they can own physical property. The owner of IP can control and be rewarded for its use, and this encourages further innovation and creativity.

The following four organisations can help direct you to most sources of help and advice across the entire intellectual property field. They also have helpful literature and explanatory leaflets and guidance notes on applying for intellectual property protection:

✔ The Intellectual Property Office (www.ipo.gov.uk)

✔ European Patent Office (http://www.epo.org)

✔ US Patent and Trade Mark Office (www.uspto.gov)

✔ World Intellectual Property Association (www.wipo.int)

I cover the most common types of intellectual property in the following sections.

Naming your business

The main consideration in choosing a business name is its commercial usefulness. You want one that lets people know as much as possible about what your company does. So choose a name that conveys the right image and message.

Whichever business name you choose, it has to be legally acceptable and abide by the rules of the Business Names Act 1985. Detailed information on this subject is available from the Business Names section at the Companies House website. Go to www.companieshouse.gov.uk and click on Guidance Booklets and then Incorporation and Names.

Looking at logos

You don't have to have a logo for your business, but it can build greater customer awareness. A logo may be a word, typeface, colour or shape. The McDonald's name is a logo because of its distinct and stylistic writing. Choose your logo carefully. It should be one that's easily recognisable, fairly simple in design and able to be reproduced on everything associated with your business. As far as the law is concerned a logo is a form of trademark (see 'Registering a trademark', later in this chapter).

Protecting patents

Patents can be regarded as contracts between inventors and the state. The state agrees with the inventor that if he is prepared to publish details of his invention in a set form and if it appears that he has made a real advance, the state will then grant him a monopoly on his invention for 20 years.

The inventor can use the monopoly period to manufacture and sell the innovation; competitors can read the published specifications and glean ideas for their research, or they can approach the inventor and offer to help to develop the idea under licence.

If you want to apply for a patent it's essential not to disclose your idea in non-confidential circumstances. If you do, your invention is already 'published' in the eyes of the law, and this could invalidate your application. Ideally, the confidentiality of the disclosure you make should be written down in a confidentiality agreement and signed by the person to whom you're making the disclosure. The other way is to get your patent application on file before you start talking to anyone about your idea. You can talk to a Chartered Patent Agent in complete confidence because they work under strict rules of confidentiality.

The process of filing an application, and publishing and granting the patent takes some two and a half years. The associated costs can be high: subject matter searches cost upwards of £500, validity searches from £1,000 and infringement searches from £1,500. The relevant forms and details of how to patent are available from the Patent Office at www.patent.gov.uk, and you can find more information in Trevor Baylis Brands' and Henri Charmasson's *Patents, Copyrights & Trademarks For Dummies* (Wiley).

Registering a trademark

A *trademark* is the symbol by which the goods of a particular manufacturer or trader can be identified. It can be a word, a signature, a monogram, a picture, a logo or a combination of these.

To qualify for registration the trademark must be distinctive, must not be deceptive and must not be capable of confusion with marks already registered. Excluded are national flags, royal crests and insignia of the armed forces. A trademark can only apply to tangible goods, not services (although pressure is mounting for this to be changed).To register a trademark you or your agent should first conduct preliminary searches at the Trade Marks Branch of the Patent Office to check that no conflicting marks are already in existence. You then apply for registration on the official trademark form and pay a fee (currently £200). Registration is initially for ten years. After this, it can be renewed for further periods of ten years at a time, with no upper time limit.

Detailing your design

You can register the shape, design or decorative features of a commercial product if it's new, original, never published before or – if already known – never before applied to the product you have in mind. Protection is intended to apply to industrial articles to be produced in quantities of more than 50.

Design registration only applies to features that appeal to the eye – not to the way the article functions.

To register a design in the UK, you should apply to the Design Registry at `https://www.ipo.gov.uk/types/design.htm` and send a specimen or photograph of the design plus a registration fee (currently £60 plus £40 for each additional design). If you want protection of your design outside the UK, you generally have to make separate applications for registration in each country in which you want protection.

Controlling a copyright

Copyright gives protection against the unlicensed copying of original artistic and creative works – articles, books, paintings, films, plays, songs, music and even engineering drawings. To claim copyright the item in question should carry the symbol © with the author's name and date.

No other action is required to take out copyright, if it's relevant to your business. For further information you can access the Copyright Service through the Patent Office website (`www.ipo.gov.uk/types/copy.htm`).

Copyright doesn't last forever. Its duration depends on the type of copyright involved and can be anything from 25 to 70 years after the creator's death.

Abiding by fair business rules

The whole way in which businesses and markets operate is the subject of keen government interest. It's not a good idea, for example, to gang up with others in your market to create a *cartel*, in which you all agree not to lower your prices or to compete with each other too vigorously.

Any such action may be brought to the attention of the Office of Fair Trading (OFT; www.oft.gov.uk). The OFT's job is to make markets work well for consumers. Markets work well when businesses are in open, fair and vigorous competition with each other for the consumer's custom.

Setting terms of trade

All business is governed by terms of trade, which are in turn affected by *contractual* relationships. Almost everything done in business, whether it's the supply of raw materials, the sale of goods and services or the hire of machinery, is executed under contract law. This is true whether the contract is in writing or verbal – or even merely implied.

Only contracts for the sale of land, hire purchase and some insurance contracts have to be in writing to be enforceable.

To make life even more complicated, a contract can be part written and part oral. So statements made at the time of signing a written contract can legally form part of that contract. For a contract to exist three events must take place:

- ✔ An offer
- ✔ An acceptance
- ✔ A consideration – some form of payment

When selling via the Internet or mail order the contract starts when the supplier 'posts' an acceptance letter, a confirmation or the goods themselves – whichever comes first.

Goods purchased via the Internet or mail order are also covered by the Distance Selling Regulations, under which customers have seven working days after they've received the goods to change their minds and return them. They don't need a reason and can get a full refund.

You must also give customers:

- ✔ Information about the company they're dealing with, such as the business name, registered and trading addresses and directors
- ✔ Written confirmation of the order – by fax, letter or email
- ✔ A full refund if their goods don't arrive by the date agreed in the original order; if no date was agreed they must be delivered within 30 days
- ✔ Information about cancellation rights
- ✔ Protection against credit card fraud

You have to meet certain standards by law for the supply of goods and services. Over and above these you need your own terms and conditions to avoid entering into 'contracts' you didn't intend. You'll need help to devise these terms. The following four basic propositions govern your conditions:

- ✔ The conditions must be brought to the other party's attention before he makes the contract.
- ✔ The last terms and conditions specified before acceptance of an offer apply.
- ✔ If any ambiguity or uncertainty exists in the contract terms they'll be interpreted against the person who inserted them.
- ✔ The terms may be interpreted as unreasonably unenforceable being in breach of various Acts of Parliament.

The Office of Fair Trading (www.oft.gov.uk) and the Trading Standards Institute (www.tradingstandards.gov.uk), can provide useful information on most aspects of trading relationships.

Describing your goods

You can't make whatever claim you like for the performance of your goods or services. If you state or imply a certain standard of performance for what you're selling, your customers have a legally enforceable right to expect that to happen. So if you state your new slimming method not only makes people lose weight but also makes them happier, richer and more successful, then you'd better deliver on all those promises.

The Trades Descriptions Acts and related legislation make it an offence for a trader to describe goods falsely. The Acts cover everything from the declared mileage of second-hand cars to the country of manufacture of a pair of jeans.

The Trading Standards Service operates at county level throughout the UK to ensure that trading laws are met. You can contact your branch by phone or via the website (www. tradingstandards.gov.uk).

Dealing with payment problems

Unless you're able to insist on payment before you send out your product or supply your service, getting paid isn't always as simple as sending out a bill and waiting for the cheque. Customers may dispute the bill, fairly or unfairly.

The Small Claims Court offers you an opportunity to collect money when you find a regular court too expensive. True, for very small cases the process isn't always cost-effective, and occasionally you have problems collecting on your judgment. But the Small Claims Court should still be part of your business's collection strategy. Check out information on the Small Claims Court at www.hmcourts-service.gov.uk.

One other route to less painful debt recovery (or problem resolution) is to go to arbitration. That is where an independent person listens to both sides of the case and makes a decision based more on common sense, fairness and practicalities than merely on the law. This is a cheaper, quicker and less intimidating process. You can find out all about the process and locate an arbitrator from the Chartered Institute of Arbitrators (http://www.ciarb.org) or its European branch (www.european-arbitrators.org).

Chapter 6

Preparing the Business Plan

● ●

In This Chapter

▶ Turning your ideas into plans

▶ Satisfying financiers' concerns

▶ Making your plan stand out

▶ Using software

▶ Preparing for an elevator pitch

● ●

*P*erhaps the most important step in launching any new venture or expanding an existing one is the construction of a *business plan.* Such a plan must include your goals for the enterprise, both short and long term; a description of the products or services you offer and the market opportunities you anticipate; and finally, an explanation of the resources and means you need to achieve your goals in the face of likely competition.

The core thinking behind business plans and their eventual implementation is strategic analysis. The strategic analysis refines or confirms your view of what's really unique about your proposition. Or to put it another way, 'Why on earth would anyone want to pay enough for this to make me rich?'

After completion, your business plan serves as a blueprint to follow that, like any map, improves users' chances of reaching their destination.

Finding a Reason to Write a Business Plan

A number of important benefits arise from preparing a business plan. All these benefits add up to one compelling reason: businesses that plan make more money than those that don't and they survive for longer too.

The research on planning generally shows a positive relationship between planning and business performance. Businesses that follow a well-thought-out plan generally out-perform businesses with no plans or informal plans in every relevant category. Businesses that continue to update their plans throughout their life enjoy significantly more success than businesses that don't.

I cover key reasons for writing up your business plan in the following sections.

Building confidence

Completing a business plan makes you feel confident in your ability to set up and operate the venture because you've put together a plan to make it happen. It may even compensate for lack of capital and experience, provided of course you have other factors in your favour, such as a sound idea and a sizeable market opportunity for your product or service.

Testing your ideas

A systematic approach to planning enables you to make your mistakes on paper, rather than in the marketplace. One potential entrepreneur made the discovery while gathering data for his business plan that the local competitor he thought was a one-man band was in fact the pilot operation for a proposed national chain of franchised outlets. This had a profound effect on his market entry strategy!

Another entrepreneur found out that, at the price he proposed charging, he would never recover his overheads or break even. Indeed, *overheads* and *break even* were themselves alien terms before he embarked on preparing a business plan. This naive perspective on costs is by no means unusual.

Showing how much money you need

Your business plan details how much money you need, what you need it for and when and for how long you need it.

Because under-capitalisation and early cash-flow problems are two important reasons for new business activities failing, if you have a soundly prepared business plan you can reduce these risks of failure. You can also experiment with a range of alternative viable strategies and so concentrate on options that make the most economic use of scarce financial resources.

To say that your business plan is the passport to sources of finance is an exaggeration. It does, however, help you to display your entrepreneurial flair and managerial talent to the full and to communicate your ideas to others in a way that is easier for them to understand so that they appreciate the reasoning behind your ideas. These outside parties could be bankers, potential investors, partners or advisory agencies. As soon as they know what you're trying to do they're better able to help you.

Providing planning experience

Preparing a business plan gives you an insight into the planning process. This process – not simply the plan that comes out of it – is itself important to the long-term health of a business. Businesses are dynamic, as are the commercial and competitive environments in which they operate. No one expects every event recorded on a business plan to occur as predicted, but the understanding and knowledge created by the process of business planning help prepare the business for any changes it may face, and so enable it to adjust quickly.

Writing Up Your Business Plan

In these sections, I give you some guidelines to make sure that your plan attracts attention and succeeds in the face of some fierce competition. More than 1,000 businesses start up in the United Kingdom each day, and many of those are looking for money or other resources that they're hoping their business plan can secure for them. Making your business plan the best it can be gives it a chance to stand out.

Choosing the right packaging

Appropriate packaging enhances every product and a business plan is no exception. Most experts prefer a simple spiral binding with a clear plastic cover front and back. This makes it easy for the reader to move from section to section, and it ensures that the document survives the frequent handling that every successful business plan is likely to get.

A letter-quality printer, using size 12 typeface, double spacing and wide margins, gives you a pleasing and easy-to-read plan.

Deciding on layout and content

No universal business plan format exists. That being said, experience has taught me that certain styles are more successful than others. Following these guidelines results in an effective business plan that covers most requirements. Not every sub-heading may be relevant to you, but the general format is robust.

The following list contains the elements of an effective business plan, one that covers most requirements. You may not need all these sections, and you may need others to cover special requirements.

> ✓ The **cover** should show the name of your business, its website, Facebook/Twitter pages, physical address, phone number(s) including a mobile, fax number(s), e-mail address, contact name and the date on which this version of the plan was prepared. It should confirm that this is the current view on the business's position and financing needs.

✔ The **title page**, immediately behind the front cover, should repeat the cover information and also give the founder's name, address and phone number. A home phone number can be helpful, particularly for investors, who often work irregular hours too.

✔ The **executive summary** is ideally one page, but certainly no longer than two, and contains the highlights of your plan. Writing this summary is a difficult task, but it's the single most important part of your business plan. Done well, it can favourably dispose the reader from the outset. If you do the executive summary badly, or not at all, then the plan may not get beyond the investor's mail room. This one page (or two pages) must explain:

  • The current position of the company, including a summary of past trading results

  • A description of the products or services, together with details of any rights or patents and of your competitive advantage

  • The reasons customers need this product or service, together with some indication of market size and growth

  • A summary of forecasts of sales and profits, together with short- and long-term aims and the strategies you'll employ

  • How much money you need to fund the growth and how and when the provider of that finance can benefit

Write the executive summary only after you complete the business plan itself.

✔ The **table of contents**, with page numbers, is the map that guides readers through the business plan. If that map is obscure, muddled or even missing, then you're likely to end up with lost or irritated readers who are in no mind to back your proposal. You should list and number each main section and give it a page number. Elements within each section should also be numbered: 1, 1.1, 1.2 and so on.

✔ Details of the **business and its management** should include a brief history of the business and its performance to date, if any, and details on key staff and their work experience, current mission, legal entity, capital structure and professional advisers.

✔ A description of **products and services**, their applications, competitive advantage and proprietary position. Include details on state of readiness of new products and services and development cost estimates.

✔ The **marketing** section should provide a brief overview of the market by major segment showing size and growth. Explain the current and proposed marketing strategy for each major segment, covering price, promotion, distribution channels, selling methods, location requirements and the need for acquisitions, mergers or joint ventures, if any.

✔ Information on **management and staffing** should give details on current key staff and on any recruitment needs. Include information on staff retention strategies, reward systems and training plans.

✔ The **operations** section describes how you make your products and services and fulfil orders, how you assure quality standards and how you can meet output.

✔ The summary of the key **financial data** includes ratios together with a description of the key controls used to monitor and review performance.

✔ Include **financing requirements** needed to achieve the planned goals, together with how long you need the money for. Also demonstrate how the business would proceed using only internal funding. The difference between these two positions is what the extra money helps to deliver.

✔ **E-commerce** isn't just about selling goods and services online, though that's important. It covers a range of activities that you can carry out online to make your business more efficient. These solutions extend across the supply chain, from ordering your raw materials right through to after-sales service. It can incorporate market intelligence gathering, customer relationship management and a whole range of back-office procedures. Your business plan should show how you plan to tackle this area.

✔ Include **major milestones** with dates. For example: get prototype for testing by 20 December, file patents by

10 January or locate suitable premises by such and such a date.

✔ **Risk assessment** features high on your reader's list of concerns, so you should anticipate as many as you can, together with your solution. For example: 'Our strategy is highly dependent on finding a warehouse with a cold store for stock. But if we can't find one by start date we will use space in the public cold store 10 miles away. This is not as convenient but it will do.'

✔ Detail an **exit route** for venture capitalists and business angels. Typically, they're looking to liquidate their investments within three to seven years, so your business plan should show them how much money they can make and how quickly.

If you think you need long-term investment (see Chapter 8 for more about equity financing), then you need to say something about who may buy the business and when you may be able to launch it on a stock market.

✔ **Appendixes** include CVs of the key team members, technical data, patents, copyrights and designs, details of professional advisers, audited accounts, consultants' reports, abstracts of market surveys, details of orders on hand and so on.

Writing and editing

The first draft of the business plan may have several authors and it can be written ignoring the niceties of grammar and style. The first draft is a good one to talk over with your legal adviser to keep you on the straight and narrow, and with a friendly banker or venture capitalist. This can give you an insider's view of the strengths and weaknesses of your proposal.

When you've revised the first draft, then comes the task of editing. Here grammar, spelling and a consistent style do matter. The end result must be a crisp, correct, clear, complete plan no more than 20 pages long. If you're not an expert writer you may need help with editing. Your local librarian or college may be able to help here.

Maintaining confidentiality

Finding an investor or a bank to lend to your business may take weeks or months. During that time, potential investors diligently gather information about the business so that they don't have surprises later about income, expenses or undisclosed liabilities. The business plan is only the starting point for their investigations.

If you and the prospective financiers are strangers to one another, you may be reluctant to turn over sensitive business information until you're confident that they're serious. (This isn't as sensitive an issue with banks as it is with business angels and venture capital providers.) To allay these fears, consider asking for a confidentiality letter or agreement.

A confidentiality letter suffices in most circumstances. But if substantial amounts of intellectual property are involved you may prefer to have a lawyer draft a longer, more formal confidentiality agreement, also known as a non-disclosure agreement (NDA). That's okay, but you (and perhaps your lawyer as well) should make sure that the proposed document contains no binding commitment on you.

You can find more information on NDAs as well as links to organisations that can help you put together an NDA at this Business Link website: www.businesslink.gov.uk> Exploit your ideas > Protecting your intellectual property > Non-disclosure agreements

Using Business Planning Software

You may consider taking some of the sweat out of writing your business plan by using one of the myriad software programmes on the market. You need to take some care in using such systems, because the result can be a bland plan that pleases no one and achieves nothing worthwhile.

Don't buy a package with several hundred business plans covering every type of business imaginable. The chances are that the person who wrote the plans knows far less than you do about your business sector and can add little or no value to your proposition. Worse still, at least an even chance exists that the reader of your plan has seen the fruits of these packaged plans before and may be less than enthusiastic to see yet another one.

Use business planning software as an aid and not a crutch. Go beyond that and you may end up worse off than if you'd started with a blank sheet of paper.

Reviewing systems

This section provides reviews of some business planning software packages and related websites that have been used to good effect:

- ✔ **BizPlanit.Com** (www.bizplanit.com; email biz@ bizplanit.com): BizPlanIt.Com's website has free resources offering information, advice, articled links to other useful sites and a free monthly newsletter, the Virtual Business Plan, to pinpoint information. It also has an email service, providing answers to business plan questions within 24 hours.

- ✔ **NatWest** (www.natwest.com/business/business-school/business-guides/planning-and-management/business-plan/default.ashx): They claim to offer a business plan in 60 seconds. They also offer some tips on writing plans and at the bottom of the page is a link to download NatWest's free business planning software.

- ✔ **Royal Bank of Canada** (www.rbcroyalbank.com/business): This site has a wide range of useful help for entrepreneurs. Click on Resource Center, then Starting a Business and then Create the Plan to access its business plan writer package and sample business plans.

- ✔ **The Royal Bank of Scotland:** The bank offers a free business plan writer to download at www.rbs.co.uk/business/banking/g2/planning.ashx#tabs=section1.

Presenting Your Plan

Anyone backing a business does so primarily because she believes in the management of the business. She knows from experience that things rarely go according to plan, so she must be confident that the team involved can respond effectively to changing conditions. You can be sure that any financier you're presenting to has read dozens of similar plans, and is well rehearsed. She may even have taken the trouble to find out something about your business and financial history.

Starring in showtime

When you present your business plan to financial backers, your goal is to create empathy between yourself and your listeners. You may not be able to change your personality, but you can take a few tips on presentation skills. Eye contact, tone of speech, enthusiasm and body language all have a part to play in making a presentation go well.

Wearing a suit is never likely to upset anyone. Shorts and sandals just set the wrong tone. Serious money calls for serious people and even the Internet world is growing up.

Rehearse your presentation beforehand, having found out how much time you have. Explain your strategy in a businesslike manner, demonstrating your grasp of the competitive market forces at work. Listen to comments and criticisms carefully, avoiding a defensive attitude when you respond.

Use visual aids and if possible bring and demonstrate your product or service. A video or computer-generated model is better than nothing.

Allow at least as much time for questions as you take in your talk. Make your replies to questions brief and to the point. If your potential investors want more information, they can ask. This approach allows time for the many different questions that must be asked either now or later, before an investment can proceed.

Making an elevator pitch

You never know when the chance to present your business plan may occur – maybe even in a lift between floors (hence the term *elevator pitch*). You need to have every aspect of your business plan in your head and know your way around the plan backwards, forwards and sideways. It's as well to have a 5-, 10- and 20-minute presentation ready to run at a moment's notice.

Chapter 7

Getting Help

. . . .

In This Chapter

▶ Locating help and advisory agencies

▶ Looking at Business Link

▶ Checking out Local Enterprise Agencies

▶ Exploring incubators

▶ Inspiring inventors

▶ Getting help for younger entrepreneurs

. . . .

*T*he fact that you've decided to start up your own business doesn't mean you have to do everything yourself. Even if you've rejected the idea of taking on a partner or going into a franchise chain, you can still get expert help and advice with nearly every aspect of your business, before you start up, while you're starting up and even long after you've established your enterprise.

Several hundred organisations are specifically concerned with providing help, advice and resources (including finance) for small businesses and those starting them. For the most part, these services are provided free or at a very low cost, at least at the outset.

Many of these organisations have been set up, or at least been encouraged to set up, by both national and local governments, who have come to realise how valuable small businesses are to communities and economies. (Chapter 2 addresses these issues in more depth.)

Although lots of people and organisations can help you get started in business, in the end you have to make the decisions. That's not to knock the great advice and wisdom that many in help agencies such as Business Link or Enterprise

Agencies and the like have to offer. However, no one can step into your shoes and see the world through your eyes. But by the same token, the final responsibility for choice of action rests with you. Listen to advice and take your own decisions.

In this chapter I introduce some of the organisations you'd be mad not to talk to if you want to get an expert outsider's view on the problems you're tussling with to get off to the best possible start.

Connecting with Government services

That the UK Government is keen to help small business should come as no big surprise. New small businesses are a key source of new jobs and eventually of tax payments. But just because the government's aims are selfish doesn't mean you shouldn't tap into any help you can get. Exactly what that help will be varies from time to time, both in terms of the type of help and its amount and form.

The contact point for access to all government help is the Department for Business Innovation and Skills website (www.bis.gov.uk). Also at the time of writing the Business Link website (www.businesslink.gov.uk) can be used to find information on the full range of advice and support for small businesses from both government and non-government agencies.

Linking to Local Enterprise Agencies (LEAs)

Local Enterprise Agencies are companies limited by guarantee, typically set up as partnerships between big companies and organisations in the private sector and local authorities, with support from central government depending on their individual circumstances. LEAs support over 100,000 pre-starts, nearly 25,000 start-ups and 130,000 established businesses – totalling over 250,000 clients – across the country every year.

Typically, LEAs directly or indirectly provide advice, information, counselling and training on a comprehensive range of business issues, as well as very often providing shared workspace with access to some business services. They're involved with all types of SMEs, including pre-starts, start-ups, sole traders, partnerships, co-operatives and limited companies.

LEAs provide business services including business counselling, training, consultancy and in some cases managed workspace.

You can find your nearest Local Enterprise Agency in the phone book, at the National Federation of Enterprise Agencies (NFEA) website, http://www.nfea.com/ www.nfea.com, or by phoning the NFEA on 01234 831621.

Choosing Small Business Associations

The services of government-supported help agencies are often free, but a growing army of commercial or semi-commercial self-help organisations is present in the field. Their basic premise is that if small firms can band together to buy goods, services or advice, or to influence government policy, they're more likely to be effective than on their own. I cover the more established of these organisations in the following sections.

The Federation of Small Businesses

The Federation of Small Businesses (FSB; website: www.fsb.org.uk; tel: 01253 336000) is a national organisation with 213,000 members that protects small firms' interests and fights for their rights. The Federation has the resources to take major test cases of importance to small business through the expensive legal process leading to the House of Lords and the European Courts if necessary. It's been particularly effective when dealing with taxation and employment matters.

For people thinking of starting their own business the FSB offers legal, environmental, fire and premises tips, as well as advice on many other issues that small business owners may have to address as the business grows. The FSB also provides information on other agencies that may be of use or assistance when starting up.

Membership costs range from £150 per annum, including a one-off registration fee of £30 for someone working on his own, up to £900 for a firm employing more than 151 people. (Prices exclude VAT.)

Amongst the valuable services on offer from the FSB is a legal benefits package, providing access to legal advice from qualified lawyers 24 hours a day, 365 days a year; tax advice from Revenue-trained specialists; information and documentation on employment, tax and commercial law; and insurance cover for legal and tax professional fees and statutory awards in the event of an employment dispute or full tax enquiry.

The British Chambers of Commerce

Though not aimed exclusively at small businesses, the British Chambers of Commerce (www.britishchambers.org. uk) offer an extensive range of services for business starters. Their national network of accredited chambers is managed and developed by their business membership and monitored at the national level to ensure that they deliver appropriate products and services to prescribed standards. They're funded by membership subscriptions.

Currently, over 135,000 businesses belong to a chamber in the accredited network, from growth-oriented start-ups to local and regional subsidiaries of multinational companies, in all commercial and industrial sectors, and from all over the UK.

British Chambers of Commerce have access to a range of benefits geared to help businesses big or small succeed and grow. With over 2,500 staff covering more than 100 locations, their network provides a ready-made management support team for any business anywhere in Britain.

Business training, information resources, networking and savings on essential overheads, all of which are tailored to individual business needs, are on offer from local chambers. Increasingly, many of their services are also available online.

The British Chambers of Commerce are also part of the global network of chambers of commerce, and for existing or potential exporters simply no better route exists to the global marketplace.

Their regular surveys, consultations and reports provide grass-roots business opinion and have strong influence on government ministers and officials, members of Parliament, and other decision makers and opinion formers.

A few more strings to your bow

Literally hundreds of organisations and associations exist thatare in the business of helping you and your businesses. Here are a few more that you should consider taking a look at to see whether their services could match your needs:

- ✔ **Association of Chartered Certified Accountants** (www. accaglobal.com) is a major accounting body. It offers 34 free fact sheets on every aspect of starting a business, including recruiting, advertising, grants, setting up an office, researching your market and effective selling (go to General Public, Technical Activities, Subject Areas, Small Business and finally Start-ups).

- ✔ **British Association of Women Entrepreneurs** (website: www.bawe-uk.org; tel: 01786 446044.

- ✔ **eBusiness Clubs** (www.ebusinessclubs.co.uk) is a free service delivered through British chambers of commerce aimed at small businesses, offering access to a range of activities including events, ICT support and information from business experts. The strapline 'How technology can improve business performance' explains the central purpose of the clubs.

- ✔ **Homeworking.com** (www.homeworking.com), started in 1999, is a resource rather than a job directory and is full of useful tips and helpful warnings about the thousands of scam businesses on offer to would-be homeworkers.

- ✔ **Livewire** (www.shell-livewire.org) is a national programme supported by Shell, an oil multinational, to help young entrepreneurs start their own businesses.

✔ **PRIME Business Club** (website: www.primebusiness club.com; tel: 0208 765 7833) claims to be the only national organisation dedicated to helping people aged over 50 set up in business. It has all the usual material on starting a business on its site, but has an emphasis on the issues older people face, such as dealing with tax credits and pensions.

✔ **The Prince's Trust** (www.princes-trust.org.uk) helps 14- to 30-year-olds develop confidence, learn new skills and get into work. It offers opportunities when no one else will. So if you've got an idea for a business but no one will give you the money to get it off the ground, the Prince's Trust may be able to provide you with finance and advice.

✔ **Telework Association** (website: www.tca.org.uk; tel: 0800 616008) costs from £34.50 a year to join. It has 7,000 members who either work or are running a business from home. You get a bi-monthly magazine, a teleworking handbook with ideas for tele-businesses and access to their help line covering all aspects of working from home.

Hotcourses (www.hotcourses.com) provide information on some 3,000 business courses run in UK colleges and universities. The company aims to be the best in the world at helping people find the course that is right for them, whatever stage they are in life. With offices in Chennai, India and London they are the largest publisher of guides to courses, colleges and universities.

Assisting Inventors

Each year over 7,000 hopeful inventors in the UK file patents to protect their intellectual property from poachers. With a success rate of getting patented ideas to market of lower than 2 per cent, inventors need all the help they can get. Check out these organisations that can smooth out the path:

✔ **The Institute of Patentees and Inventors** (website: www. invent.org.uk; tel: 0871 226 2091) has among its 1,000 members not only inventors but also patent agents, marketers and others who can provide expert advice to its membership on the complex issues relating to invention and innovation. Annual membership is £70 with a joining fee of £15.

✔ **International Federation of Inventors' Societies** (IFIA; website: www.invention-ifia.ch) has web links to its 100 member organisations and to 345 other organisations of probable use to inventors, as well as details of reference books, guides, surveys, studies, conferences, seminars, workshops, expert group meetings, lectures, competitions and awards for inventions.

✔ **NESTA** (website: www.nesta.org.uk; tel: 020 7438 2500) is the National Endowment for Science, Technology and the Arts – an independent body with a mission to make the UK more innovative. They help and invest in early-stage companies, inform policy and deliver practical programmes that inspire others to solve the big challenges of the future. They aim to bring the best ideas, new flows of capital and talented people together, and encourage them to develop them further.

Inventors often huddle together in business incubators - also known as accelerators, science parks, innovation centres, technology parks and a whole variety of other names coined over the years. These are places where new businesses can set up in a benign environment, with support services and advice close at hand. Contact either UK Business Incubation (www.ukbi.co.uk) or United Kingdom Science Park Association (UKSPA; www.ukspa.org.uk) to find out all you need to know about incubators or innovation centres that may help you achieve your ambitious goals.

Chapter 8

Finding the Money

· ·

In This Chapter

▶ Working out how much outside money you need

▶ Looking at the different types of money available to you

▶ Choosing the best source of money for you

▶ Finding money to work with

· ·

*B*usinesses need a continuous flow of customers, products or services to sell, and space to work from or store unsold goods. But they need money to make all these things happen. The more the business actually does, the more money it needs.

Even during the recent world Credit Crunch small businesses needed and, despite some anecdotal evidence to the contrary, accessed money. The latest British Banking Association (BBA; www.bba.org.uk) statistics published on 30 July 2010 showed that on a daily average basis banks were making available around £27 million of new term lending to small businesses each working day. Over the preceding 12 months, banks – the major but by no means the only source of money for new and small businesses – had lent out £54.5 billion in long and short-term loans.

This chapter helps you to find the right type of money for your business and avoid common pitfalls.

Assessing How Much Money You Need

You should work out from the outset how much money you need to get your business off the ground. If your proposed venture needs more cash than you feel comfortable either putting up yourself or raising from others, then the sooner you know the better. Then you can start to revise your plans. The steps that lead to an accurate estimate of your financial requirements start with the sales forecast, which you prepare as part of the feasibility testing that I cover in Chapter 4, along with advice on estimating costs for initial expenditure such as retail or production space, equipment, staff and so on.

Forecasting cash flow is the most reliable way to estimate the amount of money a business needs on a day-to-day basis.

Projecting receipts

Receipts from sales come in different ways, depending on the range of products and services on offer. And aside from money coming in from paying customers, business owners may, and in many cases almost certainly will, put in cash of their own. However, not all the money necessarily goes in at the outset. For example, you can budget so that £10,000 goes in at the start, followed by sums of £5,000 in months four, seven and ten respectively.

Be sure to have contingency approaches in place, in case people are late in paying you.

You should total up the projected receipts for each month and for the year as a whole. You're well advised to carry out this process using a spreadsheet program, which saves you from any problems caused by faulty maths.

A sale made in one month may not result in any cash coming into the business bank account until the following month, if you're reasonably lucky, or much later if you're not. Make sure you know the ways in which people pay their bills in the sectors of which you're working.

Estimating expenses

Some expenses, such as rent, rates and equipment leases, you pay monthly. Other bills, such as telephone, utilities and bank charges, come in quarterly.

If you haven't yet had to pay utilities, for example, put into your forecast your best guesstimate of how much you're going to spend and when. Marketing, promotion, travel, subsistence and stationery are good examples of expenses you may have to estimate. You know you face costs in these areas, but they may not be all that accurate as projections.

After you've been trading for a while, you can get a much better handle on the true costs you're likely to incur.

Total up the payments for each month and for the year as a whole.

The accounting convention is to show payments out and negative sums in brackets, rather than with minus signs in front.

Working out the closing cash balances

This is crunch time, when the real sums reveal the amount of money your great new business needs to get it off the ground. Working through the cash-flow projections allows you to see exactly how much cash you have in hand, or in the bank, at the end of each month, or how much you need to raise. This is the closing cash balance for the month. It's also the opening cash balance for the following month, because that's the position you're carrying forward.

You can check out potential customers by using a credit reference agency such as Snoop4 Companies (www.snoop4 companies.co.uk) for businesses or Experian (www.experian. co.uk) for private individuals. Basic credit reports cost between around £3 and £35 and may save you time and money if you have any reservations about a potential customer's ability to pay.

During periods of economic downturn, recessions to you and me, unsurprisingly customers take longer to settle their bills. Big firms, though perhaps a safer bet and more likely to survive, are rarely sympathetic to a small firm's plight. Expect them to go to the wire when it comes to settling up.

Research by Bacs Payment Schemes Limited (www.bacs. co.uk), the organisation behind Direct Debit and Bacs Direct Credit, published in March 2010 shows that since the Credit Crunch struck British small and medium enterprises (SMEs) are having to wait an average of 41 days longer than their original agreed payment terms before invoices are paid. That's an increase of 9.5 days compared to before the Crunch.

Reviewing Your Financing Options

Knowing how much money you need to get your business successfully started is an important first step, but it's only that – a first step. Many sources of funds are available to small firms. However, not all are equally appropriate to all firms at all times. These different sources of finance carry very different obligations, responsibilities and opportunities. You have to understand the differences to allow an informed choice.

Deciding between debt capital and equity capital

At one end of the financing spectrum lie shareholders – either individual *business angels* who put their own money into a business, or corporate organisations such as *venture capital providers* (also known as venture capitalists or VCs), who provide equity capital that buys a stake in a business. These investors share all the risks and vagaries of the business alongside you and expect a proportionate share in the rewards if things go well. They're less concerned with a stream of dividends – which is just as well because few small companies ever pay them – and instead hope for a radical increase in the value of their investment. They expect to realise this value from other investors who want to take their place for the next stage in the firm's growth, rather than from any repayment by the founder. Investors in new or small businesses don't look for the security of buildings or other assets to underpin their investment. Rather, they look to the founder's vision and the core management team's ability to deliver results.

At the other end of the financing spectrum are debt financiers – banks that try hard to take no risk and expect some return on their money irrespective of your business's performance. They want interest payments on money lent, usually from day one. They too hope that the management is competent, but they're more interested in making sure that either you or the business has some type of asset such as a house that they can grab if things go wrong. At the end of the day, and that day can be sooner than the borrower expects, a bank wants all its money back, with interest. Think of bankers as people who help you turn part of an illiquid asset such as property into a more liquid asset such as cash – for a price.

Understanding the differences between lenders, who provide debt capital, and investors, who provide equity or share capital, is central to a sound grasp of financial management.

Table 8-1 illustrates some of the differences between risk-averse lenders and risk-taking investors.

Table 8-1 Comparing Benefits of Lenders and Investors

Category	Lenders	Investors
Interest	Paid on outstanding loan	None, though dividends sometimes paid if profits warrant it
Capital	Repaid at end of term or sooner if lender has concerns	Returned with substantial growth through new shareholders
Security	Either from assets or personal guarantees	From belief in founders and their business vision

If your business sector is viewed as very risky, and perhaps the most reliable measure of that risk is the proportion of firms that go bust, then financing the business almost exclusively with borrowings is tantamount to gambling.

Debt has to be serviced whatever your business performance, so in any risky, volatile marketplace, you stand a good chance of being caught out one day.

If your business risks are low, profits are probably relatively low too. High profits and low risks always attract a flood of competitors, reducing your profits to levels that ultimately reflect the riskiness of your business sector. Because venture capitalists and shareholders generally look for better returns than they can get by lending the money, they'll be disappointed in an investment in a low-risk, low-return business. So if they're wise they don't get involved in the first place, or if they do they don't put any more money in later.

Going for Debt

You can explore borrowing from a number of possible sources in your search for outside finance. It's worth giving them all the once-over, but most people start and stop at a bank. The other major first source of money is family and friends, but many business starters feel nervous about putting family money at risk, and prefer to deal with professional financiers.

Borrowing from banks

Banks are the principal, and frequently the only, source of finance for nine out of every ten new and small businesses.

Banks are usually a good starting point for almost any type of debt financing. They're also able to provide many other cash-flow and asset-backed financing products, although they're often not the only or the most appropriate provider. As well as the main clearing banks, a number of the former building societies and smaller regional banks are competing hard for small firm lending.

Shop around for the best-buy bank just as you do for any other product or service. Check out Money Facts (http://moneyfacts.co.uk/compare/banking) or Which 4 U (www.which4u.co.uk/bank-accounts) to see who's offering the best deals.

If you import raw materials, your bank can provide you with Letters of Credit, which guarantee your suppliers payment from the bank when they present proof of satisfactory delivery. If you have a number of overseas suppliers who prefer settlement in their own currency for which you need foreign currency, cheque facilities or to buy money at a fixed exchange rate before you need it, banks can make the necessary arrangements.

Running an overdraft

The principal form of short-term bank funding is an *overdraft*. An overdraft is permission for you to use some of the bank's money when you don't have enough of your own. The permission is usually agreed annually, but can be withdrawn at any time. A little over a quarter of all bank finance for small firms is in the form of an overdraft. The overdraft was originally designed to cover the time between having to pay for raw materials to manufacture finished goods and selling those goods. The size of an overdraft is usually limited to a modest proportion of the amount of money that your customers owe you and the value of your finished goods stock. The bank sees those items as assets, which in the last resort it can use to get its money back.

The attraction of overdrafts is that they're very easy to arrange, except in the most unusual of circumstances such as during a global credit crunch. Also they take little time to set up. But their inherent weakness is that the keywords in the arrangement document are 'repayable on demand', which leaves the bank free to make and change the rules as it sees fit. (This term is under review and some banks may remove the term from the arrangement.) With other forms of borrowing, as long as you stick to the terms and conditions, the loan is yours for the duration; not so with overdrafts.

Taking on a term loan

If you're starting up a manufacturing business, you'll be buying machinery to last probably five years, designing your logo and buying stationery, paying the deposit on leasehold premises, buying a vehicle and investing funds in winning a long-term contract. Because you expect the profits on this to flow over a number of years, they need to be financed over a similarly long period, either through a bank loan or by inviting someone to invest in shares in the company – in other words, a long-term commitment.

Term loans, as these long-term borrowings are generally known, are funds provided by a bank for a number of years. The interest can be either variable – changing with general interest rates – or fixed for a number of years ahead. In some cases you may be able to move between having a fixed interest rate and a variable one at certain intervals. Unlike having an overdraft, the bank can't pull the rug from under you if your circumstances (or the local manager) change.

Going with a loan guarantee

Banks operate loan guarantees at the instigation of governments in the UK, and in Australia, the US and elsewhere. These schemes guarantee loans from banks and other financial institutions for small businesses with viable business proposals that have tried and failed to obtain a conventional loan because of a lack of security.

Currently called the Enterprise Finance Guarantee Scheme, these government-backed loans are available for periods between two and ten years on sums from £5,000 to £2.5 million. The government guarantees 70–90 per cent of the loan. In return for the guarantee, the borrower pays a premium of 1–2 per cent per year on the outstanding amount of the loan. The commercial aspects of the loan are matters between the borrower and the lender.

You can find out more about the details of the scheme on the Business Link website (www.businesslink.gov.uk; go to Finance and Grants; Finance Options; Borrowing; Loans and Overdrafts; and then Enterprise Finance Guarantee).

Cashflow Acceleration, an independent finance broker and a member of the Federation of Small Businesses, provides a free independent quotation search service for customers looking for commercial finance. At www.cashflow-acceleration.co.uk (go to Services and then Enterprise Finance Guarantee) you can see whether a bank may be prepared to lend under the scheme to your business.

Grabbing some cash locally

Many communities, particularly those operating in rundown areas in need of regeneration, have a facility to lend or even invest in businesses that could bring employment to the area. Funding from these sources could be for anything from start-up, right through to expansion or in some cases even rescue finance to help prevent a business from folding, shedding a large number of jobs or relocating to a more benign business environment.

Financing cash flow

When your business is trading two other sources of finance open up that can smooth out cash-flow troughs when dealing with business customers. Factoring and invoice discounting are both methods of funding sales after you've submitted an invoice.

Factors provide three related services:

- ✔ Immediate finance of up to 80 per cent of invoiced sales, with the balance (minus administration and finance charges) payable after a set period or when the invoice is paid

- ✔ Managing the sales ledger, including sending out invoices and ensuring they're paid

- ✔ Advising on credit risk and insuring clients against bad debts

This type of finance is provided against the security of trade debts (the amount of money customers owe you). Normally, when you raise an invoice you send a copy to the factor, who then funds up to 85 per cent against the invoice in advance of the customer paying. The remainder becomes payable either on a maturity date or when the customer pays. Because the invoice is assigned to the factor, payment by the customer is direct to the factor.

Invoice discounting operates in a similar way, except the seller retains control of its debtors and is responsible for collecting the money.

These forms of finance are directly related to sales levels and can be particularly helpful during growth spurts.

The Factors and Discounters Association (www.thefda.org.uk/public/membersList.asp) provides a list of over 40 members on its website, which has a search facility to help you define which organisations are best placed to meet your individual business requirements.

Getting physical

You can usually finance assets such as vehicles, computers, office equipment and the like either by leasing them or buying them on hire purchase, leaving your other funds free to cover less tangible expenses such as advertising or living expenses. You can use a lease to take the risk out of purchasing an asset that becomes obsolete or for taking account of repairs and maintenance costs. In return for this 'certainty' you pay a fee that's added to the monthly or quarterly charge. However, knowing the exact cost of purchasing and using an asset can be attractive and worth paying for. Hire purchase differs from leasing in that you have the option eventually to become the owner of the asset after a series of payments. Important tax implications apply to using these types of finance and you should discuss them with your accountant.

The Finance and Leasing Association Web site (www.fla.org.uk/asset/members) gives more information on the different products on offer to finance assets and has a directory of members and their contact details. You can also use the calculator at www.leasing.co.uk/leasecalculator to get some idea of the monthly repayments for different types of assets (such as software, furniture or cars) over different time periods.

Borrowing from family and friends

Those close to you are often willing to lend you money or invest in your business. This helps you avoid the problem of pleading your case to outsiders and enduring extra paperwork and bureaucratic delays. Help from friends, relatives and business associates can be especially valuable if you've been through bankruptcy or had other credit problems that make borrowing from a commercial lender difficult or impossible.

Involving friends and family in your business brings a range of extra potential benefits – but also costs and risks that aren't a feature of most other types of finance. You need to decide whether these are acceptable.

Some advantages of borrowing money from people you know well are that they may charge you a lower interest rate, you may be able to delay paying back money until you're more established and you may have more flexibility if you get into a jam. But after you agree to the loan terms, you have the same legal obligations as with a bank or any other source of finance.

Borrowing money from relatives and friends can have a major disadvantage. If your business does poorly and those close to you end up losing money, you may damage your personal relationships. So in dealing with friends, relatives and business associates be careful to establish clearly the terms of the deal and put them in writing, and also to make an extra effort to explain the risks. In short, your job is to make sure that your helpful friend or relative doesn't suffer true hardship if you're unable to meet your financial commitments.

When raising money from family and friends, follow these guidelines.

- ✔ Do agree proper terms for the loan or investment.

- ✔ Do put the agreement in writing and if it involves a limited partnership, share transaction or guarantee, have a legal agreement drawn up.

- ✔ Do make an extra effort to explain the risks of the business and the possible downside implications to their money.

- ✔ Do make sure when raising money from parents that other siblings are compensated in some way, perhaps via a will.

- ✔ Do make sure you want to run a family business before raising money from them. It's not the same as running your own business.

✔ Don't borrow from people on fixed incomes.

✔ Don't borrow from people who can't afford to lose their investment.

✔ Don't make the possible rewards sound more attractive than you would, say, to a bank.

✔ Don't offer jobs in your business to anyone providing money unless the person is best for the job.

✔ Don't change the normal pattern of social contact with family and friends after they've put up the money.

Sharing Out the Spoils

If your business is particularly risky, requires a lot of up-front finance or involves new technology, then you usually have to consider selling a proportion of your business's shares to outside investors.

However, if your business plan doesn't show profit returns in excess of 30 per cent per annum for the next three to five years (and you aren't prepared to part with upwards of 15 per cent of your business, then equity finance probably isn't for you.

A number of different types of investor may be prepared to put up the funds if the returns are good enough. I talk about each type in the following sections.

Benefiting by business angels

One source of equity or risk capital is private individuals, with their own funds and perhaps some knowledge of your type of business, who are willing to invest in your company in return for a share in the business.

Such investors have been christened *business angels*, a term first coined to describe private wealthy individuals who backed theatrical productions, usually a play on Broadway or in London's West End.

By their very nature such investments are highly speculative in nature. The angel typically has a personal interest in the venture and may want to play some role in the company – often an angel is determined to have some involvement beyond merely signing a cheque.

Two organisations that can put you in contact with a business angel are:

- ✔ The British Business Angels Association (BBAA; website: www.bbaa.org.uk).

- ✔ Angel Investment Network (www.angelinvestment network.co.uk), which operates a service matching entrepreneurs to angels. Their website also has a number of useful tools to help you get investor ready.

Alternatively, you could apply to appear on the BBC's business reality show *Dragon's Den* (www.bbc.co.uk/dragons den) and put your proposition face to face to 5 angels and 5 million television viewers.

Going for venture capital

Venture capital is a means of financing the start-up, development, expansion or the purchase of a company. The venture capitalist acquires a share of the company in return for providing the requisite funding. Venture capital firms often work in conjunction with other providers of finance in putting together a total funding package for a business.

Venture capital providers invest other people's money, often from pension funds. They're likely to be interested in investing a large sum of money for a large stake in a company.

Venture capital is a medium- to long-term investment of not just money but of time and effort. The venture capital firm's aim is to enable growth companies to develop into the major businesses of tomorrow. Before investing, a venture capital provider goes through *due diligence*, a process that involves a thorough examination of both the business and its owners. Accountants and lawyers subject you and your business plan to detailed scrutiny. You and your directors are required to warrant that you've provided *all* relevant information, under pain of financial penalties.

In general venture capitalists expect their investment to pay off within seven years. But they're hardened realists. Two in every ten investments they make are total write-offs, and six perform averagely well at best. So the one star in every ten investments they make has to cover a lot of duds. Venture capitalists have a target rate of return of 30 per cent plus, to cover this poor success rate.

Raising venture capital isn't a cheap option. The arrangement costs almost always run to six figures. The cost of the due diligence process is borne by the firm raising the money, but is paid out of the money raised, if that's any consolation. Raising venture capital isn't quick either. Six months isn't unusual and over a year has been known. Every venture capitalise has a deal done in six weeks in their portfolio, but that truly is the exception.

The British Venture Capital Association (www.bvca.co.uk) and the European Venture Capital Association (www.evca.com) both have online directories giving details of hundreds of venture capital providers. VFinance (www.vfinance.com), a global financial services company specialising in high-growth opportunities, has a directory of 1,541 venture capital firms and over 23,000 business angels. Its website also contains a useful business plan template. (See Chapter 6 for more on business planning.)

Karen Darby left school at 16 with just one GCSE. While working in a call centre in 2002 she hit on the idea of helping people find the cheapest gas, electricity and telephone companies and providing a user-friendly way to switch suppliers for free. She pitched her business proposition to Bridges Community Ventures, a venture capital firm, and raised £300,000. Three years down the road she sold her company, SimplySwitch, to Daily Mail and General Trust, leaving Karen £6 million richer.

You may find a big established business such as Cisco, Microsoft or Apple willing to provide venture capital if your business idea cuts across their field, as the story below shows.

When Alex Cassie was casting around for cash to get his new business making parts for car companies such as Aston Martin, he was steered to an apparently unlikely source, Michelin, the French tyre firm. Since 2003 Michelin has operated a scheme pledged to put £3 million into small firms near its British plants. Michelin put £20,000 into Cassie's business, which within four years employed 68 people with an annual turnover of £5 million.

Finding Free Money

Sometimes, if you're very lucky or very smart, you can get some of the money you need for free. The following sections tell you how to cash in on government grants and how winning a contest can earn you lots of lovely loot.

Getting a grant

Unlike debt, which you have to repay, or equity, which has to earn a return for the investors, grants and awards from the government or the European Union are often not refundable. So, although they're frequently hard to get, grants can be particularly valuable.

Support for business comes in a very wide variety of forms. The most obvious is the direct (cash) grant, but other forms of assistance are also available including free or subsidised consultancy, which could help you with market research, staff development or identifying business opportunities, or with access to valuable resources such as research facilities.

Keep yourself informed about which grants are available. Grants are constantly being introduced and withdrawn, but no system lets you know about them automatically. The Business Link (www.businesslink.gov.uk; go to Finance and Grants) and Grants Online (www.grantsonline.org. uk) websites can help you find out about grants.

Winning money

If you enjoy publicity and like a challenge then you can look out for a business competition to enter. Like government grants, business competitions are ubiquitous and, like national lotteries, they're something of a hit-or-miss affair. But one thing is certain: if you don't enter you can't win.

More than 100 annual awards take place in the UK alone, aimed at new or small businesses, and are mostly sponsored by banks, major accountancy bodies, chambers of commerce, local or national newspapers, business magazines and the trade press. Government departments may also have competitions for promoting their initiatives for exporting, innovation, job creation and so forth. The nature and amount of the awards change from year to year, as do the sponsors. But looking in the national and local press, particularly the small business sections of *The Times*, *Daily Telegraph*, *Daily Mail* and *The Guardian*, and on the Internet, should put you in touch with a competition organiser. Money awards constitute 40 per cent of the main competition prizes. For the most part, these cash sums are less than £5,000. However, a few do exceed £10,000 and one British award is for £50,000.

Business Match (www.businessmatch.org.uk/576.asp), the Design Council (www.designcouncil.org.uk/our-work/investment), the National Business Awards (www.nationalbusinessawards.co.uk) and the Growing Business Awards (http://gba.realbusiness.co.uk) are all websites that can help you find out about competitions.

Business Link has a Business Awards Finder (http://online.businesslink.gov.uk/bdotg/action/bafSearch). Just put in your postcode and business sector and the site provides details of any award you could be eligible to apply for. The website warns that not all the awards it flags up involve cash, but the free publicity should be more than worthwhile.

Chapter 9

Marketing Your Wares

*E*ntering the market with your product or service involves deciding on what mix of marketing ingredients to use. In cooking, the same ingredients used in different ways can result in very different products. The same is true in business, where the 'ingredients' are product (or service), price, place and promotion. A change in the way you put these elements together can produce an offering tailored to meet the needs of a specific market. For example, a hardback book isn't much more expensive to produce than a paperback. However, with a bit of clever publicity, bringing the hardback out a few months before the paperback edition and a higher price tag, the publisher can create an air of exclusivity that satisfies a particular group of customers.

Making Up the Marketing Mix

The key to successful promotion lies in knowing exactly what you want people to do. A few elements can make or break the successful marketing of your business. The elements you need to consider that go to make up the marketing mix are:

> ✔ *Place* is a general term to cover everything from where you locate your business to how you get your product or service to market. Poor distribution often explains sluggish sales growth. If your type of product gets to market

through several channels but you only use one of them, then no amount of price changes or extra promotion makes much difference.

✔ *Pricing* strategies can range from charging what the market may bear, right through to *marginal cost* (just enough to cover direct costs and a small contribution to overheads). Knowing your costs is important, but this is only one element in the pricing decision. You also have to take account of the marketplace, your competition and your product position (for example, if you offer a luxury item, your place in the market is different to that of someone who sells necessities).

✔ The *product or service* is what people use, but what they buy are the underlying benefits it confers on them. For example, when someone buys a camera she's not really considering whether it's SLR or digital, what lens it has, even what film it takes in the case of more traditional snappers – these end products aren't what customers want, what she's looking for is good pictures.

✔ *Promotion* is the means by which you will tell your market(s) about your products or services. This includes such elements as your website, leaflets, advertising and even basic items such as business cards and letterheads.

Defining Your Product or Service Parameters

To be successful in any marketplace, you need to have a clear picture of exactly what you want to do and for whom you're doing it. In other words, you need a vision and a mission.

To market your product effectively, you have to make decisions about factors such as product range and depth before you're ready to enter the market. Having decided to open a corner shop, for example, you still have to decide whether to focus on food only, or to carry household items and perhaps newspapers and flowers too. You also need to decide whether to carry more than one brand and size of each product.

If the key advantages of your corner shop are its location, opening hours, delivery service and friendly staff, all at competitive prices, then perhaps you don't need a wide or deep product range.

Using Advertising to Tell Your Story

You can't be confident that your customers share your zeal for your business proposition, so you need to convince them that they need what you're offering. The way to do this is to tell potential customers about what you're selling by advertising your wares.

The skill of advertising lies in reducing the global population to your target audience and reaching as many of them as you can at an economic cost. You first analyse the benefits or virtues of your product, isolate the features and translate these into customer benefits. Who has a need for your product? Define exactly who your potential customers are.

Question all the time. Then the advertising process is to set objectives for your campaign, decide on a budget, design the message, pick the medium to reach your target audience and determine how you're going to evaluate the success of your advertising.

When you understand the basics, which I go through in the following sections, you should also be able to analyse advertisements better, break them down into their elements and avoid the all too common mistakes that advertisers make every day.

Advertising by itself doesn't sell. It doesn't shift a bad product (or at least not more than once) or create new markets. Sales literature, order forms, a sales force, stocks, distributors and a strategy must back up your advertising.

Considering the customer's point of view

People buy a product or service for what it can do for them. Customers look for the benefits. As the seller, your mission is to answer the question 'What's in it for me?' from your potential customer's point of view.

Every time you compose a sales letter, write an advertisement or plan a trade show, you must get to the heart of the matter. Why should customers purchase your product or service? What benefit may it bring them?

You need to view all your marketing efforts from the prospect's point of view, not just your own. When you know what you're selling and to whom, you can match the features of the product (or service) to the benefits the customers can get when they purchase. A *feature* is what a product has or is, and *benefits* are what the product does for the customer. Finally, include proof that the product or service can deliver these benefits. Table 10-1 shows an analysis of features, benefits and proofs.

Table 10-1	Listing Features and Benefits	
Feature	*Benefit*	*Proof*
We use a unique hardening process for our machine.	Our tools last longer and that saves you money.	We have a patent on the process; independent tests carried out by the Cambridge Institute of Technology show our product lasts longest.
Our shops stay open later than others in the area.	You get more choice when to shop.	Come and see.
Our computer system is fault tolerant using parallel processing.	You have no downtime for either defects or system expansion.	Our written specification guarantees this – come and talk to satisfied customers operating in your field.

You can employ this format to examine the features, benefits and proofs for your own products or services and use the information to devise your ads. Remember, the customer pays for the benefits and the seller for the features. So the benefits provide the copy for most of your future advertising and promotional efforts.

Try this out on your business idea. Keep at it until you really have a good handle on what makes your customers tick. To make the process work best, you need to talk to some real prospective customers in your target market.

Making an exhibition of yourself

One way to gather useful market research data on customers and competitors is to attend exhibitions. This is also a useful way of seeing whether a demand for what you have to offer is likely to exist, because hundreds of key decision makers are gathered in one place for you to make a pitch to.

You can find out when exhibitions relevant to your business take place in the UK by searching Exhibitions UK (www. exhibitions.co.uk), the official website for the British exhibition industry, sponsored by UK Trade & Investment, the government organisation responsible for all trade promotion and development work. If you want to exhibit or attend a show overseas, TSNN (www.tsnn.com), which calls itself 'The Ultimate Trade Show Resource', operates a widely consulted event database containing data on more than 15,000 trade shows, exhibitions, public events and conferences worldwide. You need to register (free) for full access to the database.

Business Link, the British government's help agency for small businesses, has a comprehensive guide to getting the best out of exhibitions (go to www.businesslink.gov.uk, then select Sales and Marketing, Marketing and finally Trade Shows and Exhibitions). See Chapter 8 for information on finding a grant to help pay for attending exhibitions at home and abroad.

Setting advertising objectives

You're wasting your time advertising your product or service unless it leads to the opportunity for a sale in a significant number of instances. Ask yourself what potential customers have to do to enable you to make these sales. Do you want them to visit your showroom, phone you, write to your office, return a card or send an order in the post? Do you expect them to order now, or to remember you at some future date when they have a need for your services?

The more specifically you identify the response you want, the better you can tailor your promotional effort to achieve your objective, and the more clearly you can assess the effectiveness of your promotion.

The more general your advertising objective is – for example to 'improve your image' or 'to keep your name in front of the public' – the more likely it is to be an ineffective way of spending your money.

Deciding the budget

People commonly use two methods to calculate advertising budget numbers:

- ✔ **What can we afford?** This approach accepts that cash is usually a scarce commodity and advertising has to take its place alongside a range of competing demands.

- ✔ **Cost/benefit:** This approach comes into its own when you have clear and specific promotional goals. If you have spare capacity in your factory or want to sell more out of your shop, you can work out how much it costs you to increase your production and sales, and how much you may benefit from those extra sales. You then figure out how much advertising money it takes to get you the extra business.

Suppose you expect a £1,000 advertisement to generate 100 enquiries for your product. If your experience tells you that on average 10 per cent of enquiries result in orders, and your profit margin is £200 per product, then you can expect an extra £2,000 profit. That benefit is much greater than the £1,000 cost of the advertisement, so it seems a worthwhile investment.

In practice, you should use both these methods to decide how much to spend on promoting your products.

Defining the message

To define your message, you must look at your business and its products from the customer's standpoint and be able to answer the question 'Why should I buy your product?'. The best way is to consider the answer in two stages:

1. **'Why should I buy your *product or service?*'**

   The answer comes naturally when you look carefully at customers' motives for buying and the benefits they get from the product.

2. **'Why should I buy *your* product or service?'**

   The only logical and satisfactory answer is: 'Because it's better and so it's different.'

   The difference can arise in two ways:

   - You, the seller, are different. To achieve this, you establish a particular niche for your business.
   - Your product or service is different. Each product or service should have a unique selling point, based on fact.

Your promotional message must be built around the strength(s) of your product or service and must consist of facts about the company and about the product or service.

The stress here is on the word *fact*. Although many types of fact may surround you and your products, your customers are only interested in two – the facts that influence their buying decisions, and the facts of how your business and its products stand out from the competition.

The assumption is that everyone buys for obvious, logical reasons only, but of course innumerable examples show that this isn't so. Does a woman buy a new dress only when an old one is worn out? Do bosses have desks that are bigger than their subordinates' because they have more papers to put on them?

Choosing the media

Broadly, your advertising choices are *above-the-line* media, which is jargon for the Internet, newspapers and magazines, television, radio and other broadcast media, and *below-the-line* activities such as distributing brochures, leaflets, visiting cards, stationery, letterhead and the way you answer the phone.

The printed word (the Internet, newspapers and magazines) probably takes most of your above-the-line advertising budget. It's the accepted medium to reach the majority of customers. Most people read a newspaper, especially on Sunday, and magazines cater for every imaginable interest and range from parish magazines to Sunday supplements. News and articles are also increasingly available on the Internet, either as online versions of conventional papers or via blogs.

You must advertise where your buyers and consumers are likely to see your message. Your market research tells you where your likely prospects lie. Before making your decision about which paper or journal to advertise in, you need to get readership and circulation numbers and the publication's reader profile.

You can get this information directly from the journal or paper or from *BRAD* (British Rate and Data), www.brad. co.uk, which has a monthly classified directory of all UK and Republic of Ireland media. You should be able to access this through your local business library. The Audit Bureau of Circulations Electronic (www.abce.org.uk) audits website traffic, among other media, and Rajar (Radio Joint Audience Research) independently compiles radio audience statistics every quarter, providing an industry benchmark (www.rajar.co.uk). Newsgator (www.newsgator.com), and Blog Catalogue (www.blogcatalog.com) operate blog indexing services that can help you filter through the millions of blogs to let you home in on the ones that operate in your business sector.

When considering below-the-line advertising, identify what business gurus call *moments of truth* – contact points between you, your product or service and your customer. Those moments offer you a chance to shine and make a great impression. You can spot the difference at once when you get a really helpful person on the phone or serving you in a shop. The same is true of product literature that's actually helpful, a fairly rare event in itself.

Some of the most effective promotional ideas are the simplest, for example a business card with a map on the reverse showing how to find you, or thank-you cards instead of letters on which you can show your company's recently completed designs.

Writing a leaflet

Whether or not you actually use a leaflet as part of your advertising strategy, I always recommend writing one. The process forces you to think about what you have to tell potential customers about your product or service and, most importantly, what you want them to do next when they know of your existence. So if you want them to buy now, you need to give prices, availability, delivery times and so forth.

A leaflet doesn't have to be big – both sides of a sheet of A4 paper is as much as you can hope to get most readers to plough through, even if you're peddling the elixir of life. As well as carrying text, leaflets are a great way to get across more complex messages that a picture or diagram delivers best.

The rules for leaflets are that the content needs to be:

- Clear, straightforward English, simply laid out and easy to read

- Concise, using as few words as possible and jargon free

- Correct, because spelling mistakes and incorrect information destroy confidence in you and your product or service

- Complete, providing all the information needed for the reader to progress to the next stage in the buying process

Christian Aid has a useful guide to basic leaflet writing (www. christianaid.org.uk; go to Act Now, then Useful Stuff and then How to Write a Press Release)aimed at charities and pressure groups, but also useful for a small business on a tight budget. And Hewlett-Packard offers professional-looking business materials with free, easy-to-use and customisable templates for creating leaflets, flyers, brochures and advertisements (www.hp.com/sbso/productivity/howto/ marketing_main/marketing_brochure).

Using the Internet for viral marketing

The Internet is now central to the marketing process for most businesses. Even where customers don't buy online, most consumers and all business buyers check out products and services using the Internet to check price, quality and competitive offers. Increasingly, products that once had a physical presence are disappearing from the shelf. Music, software, film and now even books are available in 'soft' form to try or buy and download online.

Nine out of every ten visitors to a website arrive their via a search engine and your chances of being found depend on how your website is constructed, what words you use and where they're positioned on the page.

Viral marketing is a term that describes the ability of the Internet to accelerate interest and awareness in a product by rapid word-of-mouth communications. To understand the mathematical power behind this.

Figuring your bang-for-the-buck ratio

You should only undertake advertising where you can realistically measure the results. Everything else is self-indulgent. The formula to keep in mind is:

Effectiveness = Total cost of the advertising activity concerned ÷ Results (in measurable units such as customers, new orders or enquiries)

A glance at the advertising analysis in Table 10-2 shows how one organisation went about measuring and comparing the effectiveness of different advertising methods. Table 10-2 shows the advertising results for a small business course run in London. At first glance the Sunday paper produced the most enquiries. Although it cost the most, £340, the cost per enquiry was only slightly more than the other media used. But the objective of this advertising wasn't simply to create interest; it was intended to sell places on the course. In fact, only 10 of the 75 enquiries were converted into orders – an advertising cost of £34 per head. On this basis the Sunday paper was between 2.5 and 3.5 times more expensive than any other medium.

Table 10-2		Measuring Advertising Effect			
Media Used	Enquiries	Cost of Advert- ising	Cost per Enquiry	No. of Customers	Advert- ising Cost per Customer
		£	£		£
Sunday paper	75	340	4.50	10	34
Daily paper	55	234	4.25	17	14
Posters	30	125	4.20	10	12
Local weekly paper	10	40	4.00	4	10
Personal recom- menda- tion	20	N/A	N/A	19	N/A

Getting in the News

Getting your business into the news is one of the most cost-effective ways to get your message in front of both actual and potential customers. People see papers, TV and journals, on and offline, as being unbiased and so they have a greater impact on their audiences than pure adverts. It goes without saying that what you're looking for is favourable news. If you do have bad news coming through, check out this website: www.aboutpublicrelations.net/crisis.htm.

The surest way to get in the news is to write a press release. Better still, write lots of them. To be successful, a press release needs to get attention immediately and be quick and easy to digest. Studying and copying the style of the particular journals (or other media) you want your press release to appear in can make publication more likely.

The introduction is the most vital part. Ask yourself, 'Will what I write make the reader want to read on?' Avoid detail and sidetracks. The paragraphs should have bite and flow. Keep the sentences reasonably short. State the main point of the story or information early on.

Deciding who to contact

Remember that the target audience for your press release is the professional editor, who is the person who decides what to print. With British editors receiving an average of 80–90 press releases per week, make sure that you're publicising your latest newsworthy item, but make sure your press release is free of puffery and jargon.

Do your research to find not only the right newspapers or journals, but also the right journalists. Read their columns, or listen to or watch their programmes, and become familiar with their style and approach to news stories. Hollis (www.hollis-pr.com) publishes the details of all news contacts, listed by business area for newspapers, radio and television. Your goal is to write a press release that's so close to a journalist's own style that she has almost no additional work to do to make your news usable.

Following through

You get better results if you follow up your press release with a quick phone call. Journalists get bogged down and distracted like everyone else, so don't be too surprised if your masterpiece sinks to the bottom of a pile of prospective stories before the day is out. That phone call, or even an email if you can't get through, is often enough to keep up interest and get your story through the first sifting.

When you start getting results you want to keep the effort going. But even if you aren't successful at first, don't be disappointed or disheartened. Keep plugging away. Try to find a story regularly for the local press and get to know your local journalists and editors. Always be truthful, helpful and available. If a media contact rings you and you're in a meeting, make sure you always ring back.

Some companies always seem to get a piece in the paper every week. The stories published aren't always earth-shattering news, but the continuous drip of press coverage eventually makes an impact. For example, Virgin Airways was boosted immeasurably by successful press coverage. Few of the millions of words of copy written about Branson or Virgin have been paid for.

Using blogs and social networks

Consumers increasingly get influenced by their peer's views as to what to buy and do. This process of disseminating information was once the exclusive domain of mainstream advertising and of comment in the press or on the news. The Internet has changed the game and now everyone can find out from consumers how good or bad a product or service is.

Blogs, Facebook, Foursquare, Twitter and a host of other social networks are now an important and in some cases – such as when marketing to the under 25s – the only way to get your message across. Often more systematic processes are in place; TripAdvisor for information on hotel users' experiences is a good example, where different aspects of a hotel experience – accommodation, service, value for money – are rated on a points scale. This allows potential customers to see if the particular aspect or aspects they are looking for in a hotel are likely to be delivered.

So you need to build these social network routes into your marketing plans. Shiv Singh's *Social Media Marketing For Dummies* (published by Wiley) contains everything you need to know about this vital topic.

Selling and Salesmanship

More direct than advertising or publicity, selling is at the heart of every business. Whatever kind of selling your business involves, from moving goods over a counter to negotiating complex contracts, you need to understand the whole selling process and be involved with every aspect of it.

Telling the difference between selling and marketing

Marketing involves the whole process of deciding what to sell, who to sell it to and how. The theory is that a brilliant marketing strategy should all but eliminate the need for selling. After all, selling is mostly concerned with shoe-horning customers into products that they don't really want, isn't it? Absolutely not! Although the more effort you put into targeting the right product or service to the right market, the less arduous the selling process is, you still have a selling job to do.

The primary job of the sales operation is to act as a bridge or conduit between the product and the customer. Across that gulf flows information as well as products and services. You need to tell customers about your great new ideas and how your product or service performs better than anything they've seen to date.

Most businesses need selling and marketing activities in equal measure to get their message across effectively and get goods and services into their markets.

Selling yourself

One of the most important operational issues to address is your personal selling style. If you've sold products or services before, you may have developed a successful selling style already. If not, you need to develop one that's appropriate for your customers and comfortable for you. Regardless of your experience, assessing your selling style helps define and reinforce your business goals.

Check that you and your salespeople always see things from the customer's point of view. Review the sales styles of your salespeople to see how they can improve. Consider whether your own and your salespeople's selling styles are *consultative*, where you win the customer over to your point of view, or *hard*, where you try forcing the customer to take your product or service.

In assessing your selling style, consider the following:

- ✔ Always have a specific objective for any selling activity, together with a fall-back position. For example, your aim may be to get an order, but you may settle for the chance to tender for a customer's business. If you don't have objectives, much of your sales activity may be wasted on courtesy calls that never reach the asking-for-an-order stage.

- ✔ The right person to sell to is the one who makes the buying decision. You may have to start further down the chain, but you should always know whom you finally have to convince.

- ✔ Set up the situation so you can listen to the customer. You can best do this by asking open questions that look for long answers as opposed to closed questions that solicit a 'yes or no' response. When the customer has revealed what her needs really are, confirm these back to her.

- ✔ Explain your product or service in terms of the customer's needs and requirements.

- ✔ Deal with objections without hostility or irritation. Objections are a sign that the customer is interested enough in what you have to say at least to discuss your proposition. After you've overcome the customer's objections and established a broad body of agreement, you can try to close the deal.

✔ Your approach to closing can be one of a number of ways. The *assumptive close* takes the tack that because you and the customer are so much in agreement, an order is the next logical step. If the position is less clear you can go for the *balance sheet close*, which involves going through the pros and cons, arriving at a larger number of pros. So once again, the most logical way forward is for the customer to order. If circumstances allow, you can use the *special situation* closing technique. This may be appropriate if a product is in scarce supply or on special offer for a limited period.

✔ If you're unsuccessful, start the selling process again using your fall-back objective as the goal.

Outsourcing selling

Hiring sales people can prove to be too costly for a new or small business. A lower-cost and perhaps less risky sales route is via agents. Good agents should have existing contacts in your field, know buyers personally and have detailed knowledge of your product's market. Unlike someone you recruit, a hired agent should be off to a flying start from day one.

The big difference is that agents are paid purely on commission – if they don't sell they don't earn. The commission amount varies, but is rarely less than 7 per cent of the selling price and 25 per cent isn't unknown.

You can find an agent by advertising in your specialist trade press or newspapers such as the *Daily Telegraph* and *Exchange and Mart*. You can also try the Manufacturers' Agents' Association (MAA; website: www.themaa.co.uk; tel: 01582 767618), whose membership consists entirely of commission agents selling in all fields of business. The website has a search facility that can help you find a sales agent by geographical area, industry sector or types of customer served. You have to pay £150 plus £26.25 VAT by credit card for an MAA Net Search, allowing you to contact up to 20 agents in one search. Alternatively, trade directories list other agents' associations. However, the most reliable method is to approach outlets where you wish to sell. They know the honest, competent and regular agents who call on them. Draw up a shortlist and invite those agents to apply to you.

 The International Union of Commercial Agents and Brokers (www.iucab.org/nl) has details on some 470,000 commercial agents in Europe and North and South America.

Measuring results

Sales results can take time to appear. In the meantime you need to make sure you or your agent are doing things that eventually lead to successful sales. You should measure the following:

Activities

✔ Sales appointments made

✔ Sales calls made per day, per week, per month. Monitor trends, because last quarter's sales calls give you a good feel for this quarter's sales results

✔ Quotations given

Results

✔ New accounts opened

✔ Old accounts lost

✔ Average order size

Pricing for Profit

Pricing is another element of the marketing mix and represents the biggest decision you have to make about your business and the one that has the biggest impact on company profitability. You need to keep pricing constantly under review.

To get a better appreciation of the factors that may have an influence on what you charge, every business should keep these factors in mind.

Understanding consumer perceptions

A major consideration when setting your prices is customers' perception of the value of your product or service. Their opinion of value may have little or no relation to its cost, and they may be ignorant of the price that the competition charges, especially if your product or service is a new one.

Skimming versus penetrating

The overall image that you want to portray in the marketplace influences the prices you charge. A high-quality image calls for higher pricing, naturally. However, within that pricing policy you have the option of either setting a high price, which just *skims* the market by only being attractive to a small population of wealthier customers; or going for a low price to *penetrate* the market, appealing to the mass of customers.

Skim pricing is often adopted with new products with little or no competition that are aimed at affluent buyers who are willing to pay more to be the trendsetters for a new product. After the innovators have been creamed off the market, you can drop the price to penetrate to lower layers of demand.

The danger with this strategy is that high prices attract the interest of new competitors. If you have a product that's easy to copy and impossible to patent, you may be better off setting the price low to discourage competitors and to spread your product throughout the market quickly.

Avoiding setting prices too low

The most frequent mistake that companies make when setting a selling price for the first time is to pitch it too low. Either through failing to understand all the costs associated with making and marketing your product, or through yielding to the temptation to undercut the competition at the outset, you set your price so low that you risk killing your company.

Pondering Place and Distribution

Place is the fourth 'p' in the marketing mix. Place makes you review exactly how you get your products or service to your customers.

If you're a retailer, restaurateur or garage proprietor, for example, then your customers come to you. Your physical location probably is the key to success. If your business is in the manufacturing field, you're more likely to go out and find customers. In this case, your channels of distribution are the vital link.

Even if you're already in business and plan to stay in the same location, you may find benefit in taking the opportunity to review that decision. If you're looking for additional funds to expand your business, your location is undoubtedly an area that prospective financiers want to explore.

Choosing a location

From your market research data you should be able to come up with a list of criteria that are important to your choice of location. Some of the factors you need to weigh up when deciding where to locate are:

- ✔ If you need skilled or specialist labour, is it readily available?

- ✔ Are the necessary back-up services available, such as computer support, equipment repairs and maintenance?

- ✔ How readily available are raw materials, components and other supplies?

- ✔ How does the cost of premises, rates and utilities compare with other areas?

- ✔ How accessible is the site by road, rail and air?

- ✔ Are there any changes in the pipeline that may adversely affect trade? Examples include a new motorway bypassing the town, changes in transport services and closure of a large factory.

✔ Are there competing businesses in the immediate neighbourhood? Are these likely to have a beneficial or detrimental effect?

✔ Is the location conducive to the creation of a favourable market image? For instance, a high-fashion designer may lack credibility trading from an area famous for its heavy industry and infamous for its dirt and pollution.

✔ Is the area generally regarded as low or high growth? Is the area favourable to businesses?

✔ Can you and your key employees get to the area easily and quickly?

You may even have spotted a role model – a successful competitor, perhaps in another town, who appears to have got the location spot on. You can use its location criteria as a guide to developing your own.

Using these criteria you can quickly screen out most unsuitable areas. You may have to visit other locations several times, at different hours of the day and on different days of the week, before screening these out too.

Selecting a distribution channel

When you know where you want to locate, selecting a distribution channel involves researching methods and deciding on the best way to get your product to your customers.

Moving a product through a distribution channel calls for two sorts of selling activity. *Push* is the name given to selling your product in, for example, a shop. *Pull* is the effort that you carry out on the shop's behalf to help it sell your product. Your advertising strategy or a merchandising activity may cause the pull. You need to know how much push and pull are needed for the channel you're considering. If you aren't geared up to help retailers sell your product, and they need that help, then this may be a poor channel for you.

The way in which you have to move your product to your end customers is an important factor to weigh up when choosing a channel. As well as such factors as the cost of carriage, you also have to decide about packaging materials. As a rough rule, the more stages in the distribution channel, the more robust and expensive your packaging has to be.

Not all channels of distribution settle their bills promptly. For example, mail-order customers pay in advance, but retailers can take up to 90 days or more to pay. You need to take account of this settlement period in your cash-flow forecast.

Consider these factors when choosing channels of distribution for your particular business:

- ✔ *Does the channel meet your customers' needs?* You have to find out how your customers expect their product or service to be delivered to them and whether they need that particular route.

- ✔ *Will the product itself survive?* Fresh vegetables, for example, need to be moved quickly from where they're grown to where they're consumed.

- ✔ *Can you sell enough this way?* 'Enough' is how much you want to sell.

- ✔ *Is the channel compatible with your image?* If you're selling a luxury product, then door-to-door selling may spoil the impression you're trying to create in the rest of your marketing effort.

- ✔ *How do your competitors distribute?* If they've been around for a while and are obviously successful, you may benefit from looking at how your competitors distribute and using that knowledge to your advantage.

- ✔ *Is the channel cost-effective?* A small manufacturer may not find it cost-effective to supply retailers in a particular area because the direct 'drop' size – that is, the load per order – is too small to be worthwhile.

- ✔ *Is the mark-up enough?* If your product can't bear at least a 100 per cent mark-up, then it's unlikely that you can sell it through department stores. Your distribution channel has to be able to make a profit from selling your product too.

Part III
Staying In Business

'Good heavens – this tax investigation must
be <u>really</u> serious – You're the <u>third</u> tax
inspector to visit my little taxidermist
business this month.'

In this part . . .

Once your business is up and running the problems don't stop or slow down: They just change. Selling successfully may have looked like your biggest problem before you started out, but once you get going, recruiting and managing employees takes on at least as much importance.

Even if you make piles of profit, you have to keep alert to ways to make sure that the HM Revenue and Customs gets no more than its fair share of the proceeds. You may find that you have to manage not only your own money, but VAT (Value Added Tax), PAYE (Pay as You Earn), and NI (National Insurance).

Chapter 10

Employing People

*U*nless you intend working on your own, when running a business you're involved in employing and motivating others to do what you want them to do. Even if you don't employ people full-time, or if you outsource some portion of your work to others, you have to choose who to give those tasks to, how to get the best out of people and how to reward their achievements.

Finding Great Employees

First, you may need to change your attitude to the whole hiring process. Most entrepreneurs dislike hiring employees, so they do it as little as possible and fit it around their other 'more important' tasks.

Finding good staff is *the* number one job for a boss. You need good people to delegate to. And bringing new people into your current team can bring fresh and innovative ideas to stimulate everyone on to greater heights.

If you hope to grow your business, recruitment will become a routine task, like selling or monitoring cash flow that you do every day. Furthermore, you need a budget to carry out recruitment and selection, just as you need a budget for equipment or rent. If you don't have a recruitment budget, you shouldn't be surprised if a task for which you've budgeted no money goes wrong.

Deciding on full- or part-timers

One important decision you need to make before you can start your search for staff is whether you need to hire a full-time person. Some very good reasons may exist for not doing so. If, for example, the demand for your products is highly seasonal and has major peaks and troughs, keeping people on during slack periods may make no sense. This may be the case if you're selling heating oil, where you can expect demand to peak in the autumn and tail off in the late spring because of variations in the weather. Other examples of seasonal fluctuations are increased sales of garden furniture and barbeques in summer, and toys and luxury items before Christmas.

Using part-timers can open up whole new markets of job applicants, sometimes of a higher quality than you may expect on the general job market. Highly skilled and experienced retired workers, or women who've given up successful careers to have a family, can be tempted back into temporary or part-time work.

You can find part-time staff using the same methods as for full-time employees, which I discuss in the next sections.

Recruiting and selecting

To make sure that you get great people into your business, follow the tips in these sections.

Defining the job (s)

Set out the scope and responsibilities of the job before you start recruiting. The job description should include the measurable outcomes that you expect, as well as a description of the tasks the person is to do. So for a salesperson, spell out what the sales target is, how many calls you expect the person to make, what the customer retention target is and so on.

Too many small firms don't get round to preparing a job description until the person is in place, or worse still they don't have job descriptions at all. They argue that because jobs in the small business world have a short shelf-life because the company is growing and changing all the time, why bother? If you don't know what you want the person you recruit to be doing, then he won't know either.

Profiling the person

Flesh out your idea of the sort of person who can do the job well. If you're looking for a salesperson, then communication skills and appearance are important factors to consider, as are the person's personal circumstances, because he may have to stay away from home frequently. Make sure that you pay regard to discrimination legislation when looking at candidates' personal circumstances (I cover this in the section 'Avoiding discrimination', later in this chapter).

As well as qualifications and experience, keep in mind the person's team skills and that all too rare attribute, business savvy.

Advertising the job

You can fill positions from outside your company but also from inside it – don't overlook your existing staff. You may be able to promote from within, even if you have to provide some additional training. Also, your staff, suppliers or other business contacts may know of someone in their network who may be suitable.

You can advertise in newspapers and also on the Internet, which has a proliferation of recruitment websites and is a major source of staff.

The type of vacancy you have determines the medium that's best for you. The Internet may be right for design engineers, but a leaflet drop on a housing estate can be better when looking for shift workers.

Advertising for recruitment is subject to legal restrictions that vary from country to country. The laws most likely to apply are those relating to discrimination on the grounds of gender, race, age, religion or sexual orientation. Avoid sexist language or *he* or *she*, and select your words carefully to avoid stipulating characteristics that exclude potential applicants of a specific sex or race or in a particular age range. If in doubt, consult the Advertising Standards Authority (www.asa.org. uk) or take legal advice. Most restrictions apply to newspapers, magazines, radio and television; however, you're wise to include the Internet on that list.

Making your selection

When you have a number of applicants, first screen out the people who don't meet your specifications. Phone them if you need to clarify something, for example to establish whether they have experience of a particular software package. Then interview your shortlist, perhaps using a test where relevant to your business. Many self-administered tests are available, designed for different types of work – I talk about tests in 'Testing to find the best', later in this chapter.

If the search process has been successful you'll probably end up with more good applicants than you have time to interview. You need to evaluate all the applicants against cut-off criteria such as qualifications, experience, potential to grow with the job and travel time to work.

Set your criteria into a short-listing matrix – a table with criteria in the rows and candidates in the columns – and score candidates between one and three against each criterion, with three being a very good rating and one being barely acceptable. (The Newcastle University website at `www.ncl.ac.uk/ hr/forms/recruit` has a neat short-listing matrix that you can adapt to any job profile, as well as dozens of other useful recruitment templates.) You could set the cut-off point where applicants below a certain standard wouldn't be offered a job under any circumstances. Raise the standard if this still leaves you with an overly large list of candidates to interview.

You need to thoroughly prepare before interviewing job applicants. When interviewing, you need to:

✔ **Have a pre-prepared list of the key questions you plan to ask.**

✔ **Allow the candidate to talk freely as long as he sticks to the point.** If the candidate strays from dealing with areas on your list, bring him back by asking your questions.

✔ **Give applicants time to reply to your questions.** Don't fill every silence with another question, but if the silence persists for about ten seconds ask the candidate if he'd like you to clarify the question.

✔ **Look for specific evidence of the skills you're seeking.** Without those no possibility exists that the candidate will be suitable.

✔ **Ask questions that will give you an impression of the candidate's motivation,** such as 'What made you decide to . . .?'

✔ **Avoid asking leading questions, and be sensitive to potential discriminatory questions** (for example, age, sex, religion and ethnic group).

✔ **Avoid dominating the interview.** The candidate should be speaking for at least 75 per cent of the interview.

✔ **Close the interview on a positive note.** Leave the candidate feeling that he's had a fair hearing and has no further questions to ask. Indicate approximately when the candidate is likely to hear from you and what the next stage in the selection process is.

You may want to let the applicants meet other people in the business. This gives them a better feel for the company and you can get a second opinion on them. When Apple was developing the Macintosh, the entire Mac team was involved in every new appointment. Applicants spent a day with the team, and only when the team decided that a person was suitable did they let him in on the project.

Ideally, you end up with at least three people whom you'd be happy to appoint. Offer the job to the best candidate, keeping the others in reserve. You must have a reserve in case your first choice lets you down, accepts but then changes his mind or quits or is fired after a week or two.

Always take up references, preferably on the phone. Don't accept 'testimonials' at face value.

Welcoming new employees

Having got the right people to join you, make sure they become productive quickly and stay for a long time. The best way to do this is to have a comprehensive induction process showing them where everything is and the way things are done in your business. Keep them posted about developments – put them on the email circulation list straight away. Set them short-term objectives and monitor performance weekly, perhaps even daily at first, giving praise or help as required. Invite them to social events as appropriate.

Testing to find the best

You can supplement the classic trio of selection methods – application letter or CV, interviews and references – with other tools that can improve your chances of getting the right candidate for most of the jobs you may want to fill. These tools are often clustered under the general heading of *psychometric tests*, although most of the tests themselves have less to do with psychology than with basic aptitude.

Although tests are popular and becoming more reliable, they're neither certain to get selection decisions right nor risk free.

Dozens of commercial test publishers exist, producing over 3,000 different tests. You can locate a test and some guidance on which is best for your business needs through the British Psychological Society (`www.bps.org.uk/hopc/collarch/tests$.cfm`) or the Chartered Institute of Personnel and Development (`www.cipd.co.uk`; click on Subjects, then Recruitment and Talent Management and then Selection Methods).

Exploring Other Ways of Recruiting

You don't have to do everything involved in recruiting employees yourself. You can find a recruitment consultant or use a government Job Centre to do much of the hard work for you. In fact, they may even be better at this than you, because they recruit and select every day of the week. Research suggests that recruitment consultants, for example, are twice as successful at filling vacancies than are entrepreneurs on their own.

You could consider taking the job in question out of your business and pay someone else to do it. See 'Outsourcing jobs', later in this chapter, for more on this.

Using agencies

Occasions may well occur when you feel that you're either unable or unwilling to do the job of recruiting yourself. In such circumstances you may find it useful to use a recruitment agency. The costs involved may sound high, but when you reckon up your internal costs you may find that an agency isn't that expensive. Doing the recruiting yourself can take several days of your time and that of others in your firm. If you're working on your own or with just one or two others, this may be too great a distraction from other key tasks.

The Recruitment and Employment Confederation (www.rec. uk.com) has a searchable database of recruitment consultants listed by postcode, region and business sector. Also check out the online magazine *Recruitment Consultant* (www. rec-con.co.uk) for information and resources on many aspects of recruitment.

Using Job Centre Plus

Job Centre Plus is the government-run employment service that has professionally run offices with a growing number of staff specialising in small and medium enterprises (SMEs). Typically, the service operates out of 1,000 Job Centres based in towns where job seekers are likely to live. At any one time it has 400,000 job seekers on its database.

Job Centre Plus is particularly helpful to small firms with little experience of recruiting, because it offers a wide range of free help and advice on most matters concerned with employing people as well as signposting to other related services.

The Job Centre Plus range of services includes everything you expect of a recruitment consultant. But unlike other recruitment agencies, many of its services are free and in any event cost less than using any other external recruiter. You can find details of all its services for employers at Job Centre Plus (www.dwp.gov.uk/about-dwp/customer-delivery/jobcentre-plus).

Recruiting over the Internet

The fastest-growing route to finding new job applicants is via the Internet. The number of websites offering employment opportunities has exploded in recent years. The advantages of Internet recruitment to both candidates and clients are obvious. Internet recruitment offers a fast, immediate and cheap service compared to more traditional methods of recruitment. A number of recruitment sites have established formidable reputations in Europe and the US. These include:

- **Futurestep** (www.futurestep.com), which covers all job functions and industry sectors.

- **Monster** (www.monster.co.uk), which attracts approximately 100,000 visits per month and contains over a million curricula vitae. Its vacancies cover every industry sector and regional area.

- **Web Recruit** (www.webrecruit.co.uk), which offers to fill your vacancy through its online service for £695, or give you your money back.

Another option is to have a job-listing section on your own website. This is absolutely free, although you're certain to be trawling in a very small pool. This may not matter if the right sort of people are already visiting your site. At least they know something about your products and services before they apply.

Outsourcing jobs

If you want to, you can probably buy in almost every part of the work you do from external sources. Other companies can design and host your website and you can rent other technology. External warehouses can hold stock of your product; transport companies can deliver on your behalf; third-party call centres can handle your customer services; and online banks compete with traditional banks to offer online payment processing. You can outsource almost every other aspect of business – from accounting and recruitment, to payroll and human resource services.

Motivating and Rewarding Employees

After you've recruited the staff you want, you need to manage them in the most suitable way for your business. Management is the art and science of getting people to do what you want them to do because *they* want to do it. This is easier said than done.

Most entrepreneurs believe that their employees work for money and their key staff work for more money. Pay them enough and they'll jump through any hoop. In contrast, most research ranks pay as third or even fourth in the reasons for people coming to work.

If they don't necessarily work for money, why do people work in a particular organisation? I help provide some of the answers in the following sections.

Getting the best out of employees

My best advice for getting the best out of your employees is: get to know everyone. This may sound insane in a small firm – after all, you almost certainly recruited them all in the first place. By observing and listening to your employees you can motivate them by making them feel special.

The starting point in getting people to give of their best is to assess them as individuals and to recognise their specific needs and motivations. A person's age, gender or job influences these differences, as does the individual's personality. You need to tailor your actions to each person to get the best results.

Keeping motivation in the family

Over 80 per cent of small businesses are family businesses in which one or more relatives work in the organisation. Family businesses have both strengths and weaknesses when it comes to motivation. By being aware of them you can exploit the former and do your best to overcome the latter to give your business a better chance of prospering.

The factors that motivate or demotivate family members can be different to those affecting non-family members.

The overwhelming strength of a family business is its different atmosphere and feel. A sense of belonging and common purpose usually leads to good motivation and performance. Another advantage is that a family firm has greater flexibility, because the unity of management and shareholders provides the opportunity to make quick decisions and to implement rapid change if necessary. On the downside, several weaknesses exist. Although these weaknesses aren't unique to family businesses, family firms are particularly prone to them.

Rewarding achievements

Different types of work have different measurable outcomes. You need to identify the outcomes you want and arrive at a scale showing the base rate of pay and payment above that base for achieving particular objectives. Different types of 'payment by results' schemes are in common use and to make sure you pick the right mix of goals and rewards, examine carefully the conditions that most favour these types of pay.

Setting pay scales

People don't come to work just for money, but they certainly won't come if you don't pay them, and they won't stay and be motivated to give of their best if you don't give them the right pay. But how much is the right amount? Get it too low and you impair your ability to attract and retain productive and reliable people capable of growing as your business grows. But pay too much and your overheads rise so high that you become uncompetitive. Small firms face the very real danger of a wage bill that represents their largest single business expense.

The ground rules for pay aren't very complicated but they are important:

> ✔ Pay only what you can afford. Don't sink the company with a wage bill that it can't meet.

✔ Make sure that pay is fair and equitable and that every-one sees it as such.

✔ Make sure that people know how you arrive at your pay scales.

✔ See that pay scales for different jobs reflect the relative importance of the job and the skills required.

✔ Ensure that your pay scales are in line with the law on minimum wage requirements. The UK has a *statutory minimum wage*, the amount of which is governed by the age of the employee and whether an employee is undergoing training. The hourly rate changes over time, so you need to keep abreast of the latest rates (www.hmrc.gov.uk/nmw has information on current rules in this area).

✔ Ensure that your pay scales are competitive with those of other employers in your region or industry. PayScale (www.payscale.com/hr/default) is a site where you can get accurate real-time information on pay scales.

Ways to find out the going rate for a job include:

✔ Read articles on pay, as well as job advertisements on the Internet, in local papers and in the relevant trade journals. You may have to correct some pay rates to allow for variations. For example, pay rates for similar jobs are often much higher in or near major cities than they are in rural areas.

✔ Talk to your chamber of commerce or trade association, some of which publish salary surveys, and to other local employers and business owners in your network.

✔ Contact employment agencies, including those run by the government. They're usually a bit ahead of the rest of the market in terms of pay information. Other employers know only what they're paying their present staff. Recruitment agencies know what you have to pay to get your next employee.

Deciding the pay rates of people who work for you arbitrarily may appear to be one of the perks of working for yourself. But inconsistent pay rates quickly upset people and staff members tend to jump ship at the first opportunity.

Matching pay to performance

You may want to add to people's salaries by rewarding them with money or benefits for the level of performance they achieve. I discuss various reward approaches in this section, which all follow the same ground rules for matching pay to performance:

✔ Make the rules clear so that everyone knows how the reward system works.

✔ Make the goals to be achieved specific and if possible quantifiable.

✔ Make the reward visible so that everyone knows what each person or team receives.

✔ Make the reward matter. It has to be worthwhile and commensurate with the effort involved.

✔ Make the reward fair, so that people believe it's correctly calculated.

✔ Make the goals realistic, because if you set the target too high no one will try to achieve it.

✔ Make the reward happen quickly.

Paying a commission

This is perhaps the easiest reward system, but it really only works for those directly involved in selling. A *commission* is a payment based in some way on the value of sales that the individual or team concerned has secured.

You have to make sure that the order is actually delivered or executed before you pay any commission and you may even want to make sure that the customer has paid up. However, as with all rewards, you must keep the timescale between doing the work and getting the reward as short as practicably possible, otherwise people forget what the money is for.

Base the commission on your gross profit (the value of sales less the cost of generating those sales) rather than your sales turnover – otherwise you can end up rewarding salespeople for generating unprofitable business.

Awarding bonuses

A *bonus* is a reward for successful performance, usually paid in a lump sum related as closely as possible to the results that an individual, team or the business as a whole has obtained. In general, bonuses are tied to results, so that how an individual contributed directly to the result achieved is less obvious. For example, a company bonus may be paid to everyone if the firm as a whole achieves a certain level of output. Keeping everyone informed about how the firm is performing towards achieving that goal may well be motivational, but the exact role that, say, a cleaner or office worker has in helping to attain that goal isn't easy to assess – not as easy as it is to calculate a salesperson's commission.

You can pay bonuses periodically or as a one-off payment for a specific achievement.

Sharing profits

Profit sharing involves giving a specific share of the company's profit to its employees. The share of the profits can be different for different jobs, length of service or seniority.

This type of reward has the great merit of focusing everyone's attention on the firm's primary economic goal – to make money. One or more employees can be performing well while others drag down the overall performance. In theory, in such circumstances the high-performing staff put pressure on the others to come up to the mark.

If profits go up, people get more; but profits can also go down, which can be less attractive. Also, the business can miss profit targets for reasons outside of employees' direct control. If your company depends on customers or supplies from overseas, for example, and the exchange rate moves against you, profits, and hence profit-related pay, can dip sharply. However unfair this may seem to a receptionist who's been hoping for extra cash to pay for a holiday, this is the hard reality of business. If you think your employees are adult enough to take that fact on board, then profit sharing can be a useful way to reward staff.

Sharing ownership

Share option schemes give employees the chance to share in the increase in value of a company's shares as it grows and prospers.

The attraction of turning employees into shareholders is that doing so gives them a long-term stake in the business, hopefully makes them look beyond short-term issues and ensures their long-term loyalty. Of course, unwelcome side effects can occur if the value of the business goes down rather than up. Share schemes also have some important tax implications that you need to take into account. You can find out all about these on the HM Revenue and Customs website (www.hmrc.gov.uk/shareschemes).

Giving skill and competence awards

You can give a skill or competence award when an employee reaches a certain level of ability. These awards aren't directly tied to an output such as improved performance, but you must believe that raising the skill or competence in question ultimately leads to better business results.

The award itself can be cash, gift certificates, extra days of holiday, a trip to a show or sports event or whatever else your employees may appreciate. Bottles of wine always seem to be well received!

Staying on the Right Side of Employment Law

All businesses operate within a legal framework, the elements of which the owner-manager must be aware. The areas I cover in the following sections summarise only a few of the key legal issues. Different types of business may have to consider different legal issues and employment law itself is dynamic and subject to revision and change.

The Advisory, Conciliation and Arbitration Service (ACAS; www.acas.org.uk) and the British Safety Council (www.britishsafetycouncil.org) are useful organisations that can help with aspects of employment issues. Emplaw (www.emplaw.co.uk) is a website covering basic British employment law information and can direct you to a lawyer in your area who specialises in the aspect of employment law you're concerned with.

Keeping employment records

You need to keep records about your employees, both individually and collectively. Keeping proper records makes the process of employing people run more smoothly. Some of the data you need to keep is a legal requirement, such as information on accidents. Some of the information is also invaluable in any dispute with an employee, for example in a case of unfair dismissal.

The individual employee information you retain should include:

- ✔ Application form
- ✔ Interview record and results of any selection tests used
- ✔ Job history, including details of promotions and assignments
- ✔ Current and past job descriptions
- ✔ Current pay and bonus details and a record of the amount and date of any changes
- ✔ Details of skills and competences
- ✔ Education and training records, with details of courses attended
- ✔ Details of performance assessments and appraisals
- ✔ Absence, lateness, accident, medical and disciplinary records, together with details of any formal warnings and suspensions
- ✔ Holiday entitlement
- ✔ Pension contribution data
- ✔ Termination record giving date, details of exit interview and suitability for re-engagement
- ✔ Copies of any correspondence between you and the employee

Collective information should include:

- ✔ Numbers of staff, grades and job titles
- ✔ Absenteeism, staff turnover and lateness statistics
- ✔ Accident rates
- ✔ Records on age and length of service
- ✔ Wage and salary structures
- ✔ Employee costs
- ✔ Overtime statistics showing hours worked and costs
- ✔ Records of grievances and disputes
- ✔ Training records showing how many person days have been devoted to training and how much that's cost
- ✔ Gender, ethnic and disability profiles

Employees have three basic rights over the information an employer keeps in their employment records:

- ✔ To be able to obtain access to their personal data
- ✔ To be able to claim damages for losses caused by the use of inaccurate data or the unauthorised use of data, or by the loss or destruction of data
- ✔ To apply to the courts if necessary for rectification or erasure of inaccurate data

This means that an employee is entitled to gain access to his personal data at reasonable intervals and without undue delay or expense. This request must legally be put in writing, although you may choose not to insist on this, and you must provide the information within 40 days of the request.

Preparing contracts of employment

You have to give an employee a written statement of certain terms and conditions of his employment within two months of his starting working for you.

The list of terms that form part of this statement include the following:

- ✔ The employee's full name

- ✔ When the employee started working for you

- ✔ How and how much you pay your employee

- ✔ Whether pay is weekly or monthly

- ✔ The hours you expect the employee to work

- ✔ The number of days' holiday the employee is allowed, including public holidays, and how that holiday is accumulated

- ✔ The employee's job title or a brief description of his work

- ✔ Where you expect the employee to work and what conditions apply if you expect him to work elsewhere

- ✔ You need to state whether you intend the employment to be permanent or, if it's for a fixed term, when it starts and finishes

- ✔ Details of who manages the employee and whom he can talk to if he has any dispute with that person

- ✔ Any terms and conditions relating to sickness or injury, including any provision for sick pay

- ✔ Any terms and conditions relating to pensions and pension schemes

- ✔ Any disciplinary rules applicable to the employee

- ✔ The period of notice required, which increases with length of service; a legal minimum of one week's notice per year of service is required up to a maximum of 12 weeks (express terms in the contract may override this)

The job description forms the cornerstone of the contract of employment that exists between employer and employee. However, the contract is rarely a single document and may not even be completely documented. A contract comes into existence as soon as someone accepts an offer of paid employment, even if both offer and acceptance are only verbal. In practice, the most important contractual document may be the letter offering the person the job, and detailing the salary and other basic employment conditions. Many employers don't document the contractual relationship with employees properly and end up with disputes. ions, for example.

Working legally

Although the owner of a business may be content to work all hours and in any conditions the law strictly governs most aspects of how you must treat employees, both prospective ones and those you appoint. Also as an employer, you must keep records that show you comply with the rules. These websites will help you keep up to speed with this field:

- ✔ The Business Link website has information on everything you need to meet your obligations as an employer when it comes to taking on staff (www.businesslink. gov.uk; go to Employment and Skills, then Becoming an Employer and then Taking on a New Employee).

- ✔ The Directgov website has information on everything you need regarding working hours (www.direct.gov. uk; click on Employment, then Employment Terms and Conditions and then Working Hours).

- ✔ The Emplaw website (www.emplaw.co.uk) has a free area covering the current regulations in British employment law, and also details on how you can find a lawyer in your area who specialises in the aspect of employment law you're concerned with.

- ✔ The Health and Safety Executive website (www.hse. gov.uk) has a section devoted to small firms, covering both regulations and advice on making your work environment safer.

- ✔ Work Smart, a Trade Union Council-run website, has a full description of the latest rules and regulations on these ever-changing topics. (Go to www.worksmart. org.uk, click on Your Rights and then Working Life and Family-friendly Policies.)

Chapter 11

Operating Effectively

· ·

In This Chapter

▶ Selecting premises

▶ Opting to make it yourself or buy from outside

▶ Choosing and using suppliers

▶ Looking at operating risks

▶ Delving into directors

▶ Deciding on key business advisers

· ·

*A*lthough you've decided to go into business, it doesn't necessarily mean that you have to make your own product, carry out every aspect of the business yourself or even work from a dedicated premises. The best use of your time may be to outsource the most time-consuming and least valuable aspect of your business. For example, I bet you can't get a package from Milton Keynes to Penzance in under 24 hours and see change from a £20 note! But a delivery service can.

Whether you buy in most of what you sell, or just some components and assemble them yourself, you have to choose between the dozens if not hundreds of suppliers in the market. Price alone is rarely a good enough guide to which supplier to choose. If they can't deliver on time, price is irrelevant.

You have to face risks in your business, not all of which you either want to or are able to shoulder yourself. For these you have to make choices about insurance types and levels to cover you. Even if you're a director of your limited company, some of those company risks fall on you and the consequences of getting things wrong can be serious, even catastrophic.

Fortunately, you don't have to face all these decisions alone. Plenty of advisers are there to help. This chapter looks at the decisions and risks involved in running a business and helps you to choose someone to help you through the minefield.

Proposing Premises

If you can avoid taking on premises when starting up your business, perhaps by working from home, so much the better. (See 'Working from home' in Chapter 3 for more information.) If that's not an option, read on.

Buying or leasing, the term used for renting a business premises, entails navigating through a number of important and often complex regulations, as well as the practical nuts and bolts of finding, fitting out and settling in to the premises. These regulations go way beyond the scope of the physical premises into areas such as opening hours and health and safety.

Calculating requirements

The first decision to make is how much space you actually require and what other facilities you need. The space is the easy bit. You can take the steam age route and make cut-out scale models of the various items you need – chairs, desks, tables and so forth – and set them out on scaled drawings of the premises. By a process of trial and error you should be able to arrive at an arrangement that's flexible, convenient to work in and meets the needs of customers and staff alike. You can also take the high-tech route and use a software program to save on the scissor work. Try Google's free program Sketchup (http://sketchup.google.com), a 3D modelling software tool that's easy to learn and simple to use. Alternatively, for around £90 you can buy a package from Smart Draw (www.smartdraw.com/specials/officeplanning.asp); you can try for free before you buy.

Finding the right premises

As soon as you know where you want to be, how much space you need and any special requirements, you can hit the trail visiting local estate agents, reading the local press and generally keeping your ear to the ground. You can, of course, get someone else to do much of the donkey work for you and put your valuable time to more productive work such as finding customers or raising dosh. Office Planet (www.office-planet. net) and Official Space (www.officialspace.co.uk), for example, provide free office-finding services. You can search through their databases of available properties and create a shortlist of solutions that meet your needs, or simply call an adviser.

If you're looking for a workshop, warehouse or showroom that doesn't have to be in the centre of a town, Ashtenne (www.ashtenne-online.co.uk; an Industrial Fund Unit Trust that owns 500 industrial estates around the UK ranging in size from 500 to 50,000 square feet) and Comproperty (www. comproperty.com) operate online databases for buying, selling or leasing commercial property and businesses in the UK.

For retail premises, Shop Property (www.shopproperty.co.uk) and Daltons Business (www.daltonsbusiness.com) have online databases of shops for sale and rent, searchable by price, size and location throughout the UK.

Renting or owning?

This is another of those imponderable questions. Buying a premises gives you all sorts of advantages, not least that you can make any alterations you want (if the law allows) without going cap in hand to a landlord, and of course no one can kick you out. On the downside, you have to invest a substantial amount of money up front and you have to sell up if you outgrow the premises. You of course enjoy any rise in the value of the property, but if you really believe that property is a better bet than investing in your own business, perhaps you should rethink your business proposition.

Renting isn't without its problems, however. You have to take on the property for a number of years and even if you sublet with the landlord's permission, you're liable for rent for the full period should the person you sublet to default. Rents are reviewed, almost invariably upwards, every three to seven years. You're expected to keep the property in good repair and return it to the landlord at the end of the lease period in the condition it was at the outset. That can prove expensive if the landlord doesn't share your opinion that any changes you've made constitute an improvement.

Net Lawman (`www.netlawman.co.uk/info/business-property-lease.php`) provides free advice and information to both landlords and tenants about business leases. Also, the Communities and Local Government website has a guide to the law governing commercial property leases (`www.communities.gov.uk/publications/regeneration/business tenancies`).

Sorting out equipment

After you've found the right premises you need to furnish them. A number of items such as furniture, shelving, filing and computing equipment are common to many types of business. Some require more specialised items, including cookers, commercial printers and machine tools. Only in the most exceptional cases should a start-up business buy new equipment. Aside from the basic economics – new may cost two to three times as much as used – until you get trading you have no real idea of what you actually need.

These are useful sites, apart from the ubiquitous eBay, on which to search out second-hand business equipment:

- ✔ Auction Guide (www.auctionguide.com)
- ✔ Greasy Machines (`www.greasymachines.com`)
- ✔ MM Börse Online (`www.mm-boerse.de`)
- ✔ Office Furniture Desks and Chairs (`www.office furnituredesksandchairs.co.uk`)

Searching for suppliers of new products is best done using a business-to-business directory, such as those provided by Business Magnet (`www.businessmagnet.co.uk`), Kelly Search (`www.kellysearch.co.uk`) and Kompass (`www.kompass.co.uk`), which between them have global databases of over 2 million industrial and commercial companies in 200 countries, listing over 200,000 product categories. You can search by category, country and brand name.

Setting quality standards

Quality may well be, like beauty, in the eye of the beholder, but you're wise to set clear standards that you expect every aspect of your end product or service to conform to. This is true whether you make in-house or outsource.

A number of well-regarded quality standards may help you monitor and control your quality. The BS EN ISO 9000 series provides perhaps the best-known standards. They can ensure that your operating procedure delivers a consistent and acceptable standard of products or services. If you're supplying to large firms they may insist on your meeting one of these quality standards, or on auditing your premises to satisfy themselves. The British Standards Institute (`www.bsi-global.com`) can provide details of quality standards.

A number of commercial organisations provide user-friendly guidelines and systems to help you reach the necessary standard. Searching the web using keywords such as *Quality standards* or *Measurement* brings up some useful sites.

Choosing a Supplier

Selecting the wrong supplier for your business can be a stressful and expensive experience. This section offers some pointers on how to find a supplier and make sure that your supplier can meet your business needs.

Look for value in the service a supplier offers rather than just the price you pay. The key questions you should ask about any prospective suppliers to your business are:

- ✔ Do they offer a guaranteed level of service?

- ✔ Do they have a strong business track record and evidence of financial stability? Check out their accounts at Companies House (`www.companieshouse.gov.uk`).

- ✔ Do they have clients in your business sector and local area?

✔ Can they provide you with client references and impartial evidence of their quality? You should check out references to make sure that suppliers are reliable and can meet deadlines.

✔ Can they meet rushed deliveries in case of emergency?

✔ What level of after-sales support do they provide?

✔ Do they offer value for money when compared to competitive services?

✔ Do you think you can enjoy working with them? If so, the relationship is going to be more productive.

Thomas's Register (www.thomasnet.com), Kelly's (www.kelly.co.uk) and Kompass (www.kompass.com) between them have details on over 1.6 million British companies and hundreds of thousands of American and Canadian manufacturers, covering 23 million key products and 744,000 trade and brand names. If someone makes a particular product, you can find their details in one of these directories.

Some free search facilities are available online. Your local business library also holds hard copies of directories and may even have Internet access to all the key data you may ever need on suppliers.

Evaluating trading terms

Buying is the mirror image of selling. Remember that as you negotiate with suppliers, who are essentially selling their services. Even if they have no deliberate intention to mislead, you may be left thinking that a supplier isn't committed to doing what you want in the way you want it. So get any agreement in writing.

The starting point in establishing trading terms is to make sure that suppliers can actually do what you want and what they claim to be able to do. This involves checking them out and taking up references.

The next crunch point is price. As a small business you may feel you're fairly short on buying power. That may be true, but room for negotiation always exists. All suppliers want more customers and sometimes they want them badly enough to shift on price.

If you do your research by contacting several suppliers so that you have a good idea of the price parameters before you talk seriously to any supplier, set yourself a target discount price and start negotiating 10 per cent or so below that. In any negotiation you may well have to give ground, so if you start at your target price you end up paying more.

You need to examine all the contract terms, such as delivery, payment terms, risk and ownership (the point at which title to the goods passes from the maker to you), warranties and guarantees, termination, arbitration rules if you fall out and the governing law in dealings with overseas suppliers. These issues are the same ones you deal with when you set your own terms of trade.

Buying online

Buying online has a range of important benefits for a small firm. Big companies have buying departments whose job is to find the best suppliers in the world with the most competitive prices and trading terms. A small firm can achieve much the same at a fraction of the cost by buying online – it can lower costs, save scarce management time and get supplies just in time, hence speeding up cash flow and reducing stock space, along with a range of other benefits.

The range of goods and services that you can buy online is vast and getting larger. As well as office supplies you can buy computer equipment, software, motor vehicles, machine tools, vending equipment, insurance, hotel accommodation, airline tickets, business education, building materials, tractors, work clothing and cleaning equipment, to name but a few.

You can use several methods to buy business supplies online. I explain the most useful methods in the following sections.

Joining an e-buying group

Online buying groups go by various names, including trading hubs, e-marketplaces, online communities, aggregators and cost reducers.

Buying in this way allows you to collect information from potential vendors quickly and easily. These online markets gather multiple suppliers in one place so that you can comparison shop without leaving your office or picking up the phone. For example, if you need to buy toner cartridges for your office laser printer, you can go to an online marketplace and search the catalogues of multiple office supplies vendors, buying from the one that offers the best deal. You can also do this for bigger-ticket items such as office furniture or photocopiers. No more calling a handful of potential suppliers, sitting through sales presentations and negotiating prices. Comparison shopping saves you time for more valuable business activities and gets you a better rate.

Buying Groups (www.buyinggroups.co.uk) offers an online guide to British buying groups and purchasing consortia. Also, e-Three (www.e-three.com) offers a service to facilitate collaboration with other organisations to leverage purchasing volumes and so secure more competitive prices and terms.

Going in for auctions

Online auctions are another way to buy supplies online. Their advantage is that you pay only as much as you're willing to. The disadvantage is that you may have to wait for the right deal to come up.

Auctions are a great way to significantly reduce the funds you need to purchase items on your business *wish list* – items you want now or need eventually but that aren't a current necessity. (See 'Sorting out equipment', earlier in this chapter.)

Bartering online

You can avoid using hard cash by taking advantage of online barter exchanges. These e-exchanges let you trade your company's products and services for those of other businesses. You can swap ad space for accounting services, or consulting for computers. For start-ups or cash-strapped companies, barter can be an effective way to get products or services you may otherwise be unable to afford. An organisation that can help you get started with bartering is Bartercard (website www.bartercard.co.uk; tel. 0845 219 7000).

Minimising Risk and Assessing Liability

As the saying goes, no pain, no gain. Some of the pain is routine and you can allow for it in the normal course of events. Employees come and go, you have to pay suppliers, you have to move into and out of premises. But some events are less easy to predict and can have serious if not disastrous consequences for your business. What happens if the warehouse burns down or your pizzas send a few customers to hospital?

You can't be expected to know that such things will happen ahead of time, but you can be reasonably sure that *something* will happen *sometime.* The laws of probability point to it and the law of averages gives you a basis for estimating your chances. You have to be prepared to deal with the unexpected, which is what this section helps you do.

Insurance forms a guarantee against loss. You must weigh up to what extent your business assets are exposed to risk and what effect a particular event may have on the business if it occurs.

 One very simple way to assess risk is to get an insurance quote to cover the risk. Insuring against an earthquake in London is very cheap, but the same cover in Istanbul costs a significant sum.

Insurance is an overhead, producing no benefit until a calamity occurs. How much insurance to carry is therefore a commercial decision, and although the temptation exists to minimise cover, you should resist it. You must carry some insurance cover, either by employment law or as an obligation that a mortgager imposes.

Establish your insurance needs by discussing your business plans with an insurance broker. Make sure that you know exactly what insurance you're buying; and, because insurance is a competitive business, get at least three quotations before making up your mind.

The Association of British Insurers (ABI; www.abi.org.uk) and the British Insurance Brokers' Association (BIBA; www.biba.org.uk) can put you in touch with a qualified insurance expert.

Protecting your employees

You must carry at least £2 million of liability insurance to meet your legal liabilities for death or bodily injury incurred by an employee during the course of business. In practice, this cover is usually unlimited, with the premiums directly related to your wage bill.

Employer's liability covers only those accidents in which the employer is held to be legally responsible. You may want to extend this cover to any accident to an employee while on your business, whoever is at fault. You may also have to cover your own financial security, particularly if the business depends on your being fit and well.

Covering yourself against an employee suing

The advent of no-win, no-fee legal support is encouraging more individuals to feel confident enough to take on companies both big and small, and often in circumstances where their chances of success aren't immediately obvious.

The growing burden of employment legislation facing small firms is forcing more and more businesses to take out legal expense insurance as the risk for being prosecuted for breaking the law rises.

But not only the risk is rising. The consequences of breaking the law are spiralling upwards too. The ceiling for unfair dismissal awards has risen from £50,000 with the maximum sum recently awarded of £84,005, just one example of the burden of new employment laws. In 2009 some 52,711 unfair dismissal claims were filed, up from 40,941 the previous year.

 The Job Rights website has an unfair dismissal calculator. (www.jobrights.co.uk/unfair-dismissal-calculator.htm). Just put in age, years of service, pay and a number of other factors including how long it might take for the person to get another job and – hey presto! – a number appears. The figure may not match the actual bill when it comes in, because the law is an uncertain arena. But it gives you something to work with from a budgeting perspective.

The remedy for the small firm without its own human resources department to keep it operating clearly within legal boundaries and a legal department to fend off any legal threats is to take out legal expenses insurance.

Firms that sign up for this type of insurance can not only expect the insurance company to pay any fines and awards they incur, but also their costs associated with defending themselves against allegations.

Protecting assets

Obviously, you need to insure your business premises, plant and equipment. However, you can choose between a couple of ways to do that:

- ✔ **Reinstatement** provides for full replacement cost.
- ✔ **Indemnity** meets only the current market value of your asset.

You also have to consider related costs and coverage. For example, who pays for removing debris? Who pays the architect to design the structure if you have to rebuild? Who reimburses employees for any damaged or destroyed personal effects? And potentially the most expensive of all: who covers the cost of making sure that a replacement building meets current, possibly more stringent and more expensive, standards?

The small print of your insurance policy covers these factors, so if they matter to your business check them out.

From raw materials through to finished goods, stock is as exposed as your buildings and plant in the event of hazards such as fire and theft. Theft from commercial property runs to hundreds of millions of pounds per annum.

When you're in business you can expect threats from within and without. You can take out a *fidelity guarantee*, the name of this particular type of insurance, to protect you from fraud or dishonesty on the part of key employees. You can also take out normal theft cover to protect your business premises and their contents.

Covering loss of profits

Meeting the replacement costs of buildings, plant, equipment and stock doesn't compensate you for the loss of business and profit arising out of a fire or other disaster. Your overheads, employees' wages and so on may have to continue during the period of interruption. You may incur expenses such as getting subcontracted work done. Insurance for *consequential loss*, as this type of insurance is known, is intended to restore your business's finances to the position they were in before the interruption occurred.

Goods in transit

Until your goods reach your customers and they accept them, the goods are still at your risk. You may need to protect yourself from loss or damage in transit.

Protecting yourself

Anyone who puts a substantial amount of money into your business – a bank or a venture capitalist, for example – may require you to have *key man insurance*. This type of insurance provides a substantial cash cushion in the event of your death or incapacity – you being the key man (even if you're a woman) on whom the business's success depends.

Key man insurance is particularly important in small and new firms where one person is disproportionately vital in the early stages. In a partnership, your partners may also consider this a prudent protection.

Guaranteeing goods and services

As well as your own specifications confirming how your products or services perform, you may have legal obligations under the *Consumer Protection Act*, which sets out safety rules and prohibits the sale of unsafe goods; and the *Sale of Goods Acts*, which govern your contractual relationship with your customer. In addition, the common-law rules of negligence also apply to business dealings.

If you're a principal in a partnership with unlimited liability, a lawsuit concerning product liability is quite likely to bankrupt you. Even if you carry out the business through a limited company, although the directors may escape personal bankruptcy, the company doesn't. If you believe that real risks are associated with your product, then you need to consider taking out product liability insurance.

If your business involves foodstuffs, you must also pay close attention to the stringent hygiene regulations that now encompass all food manufacture, preparation and handling. If you've thoroughly examined and identified all the hazard points yet something unforeseen goes wrong, you can claim the defence of 'due diligence', in so far as you've done everything you could reasonably have been expected to do. Trading Standards (www.tradingstandards.gov.uk) and environmental health officers based in your local government office are there to help and advise in a free consultative capacity.

Producers or importers of certain types of goods face obligations under both the Consumer Protection Act 1987 and the Sale of Goods Act 1979. Importers can be sued for defects; they can't disclaim liability simply because they haven't been involved in manufacture.

 Business Link can give you the low-down on this subject. Go to its website at www.businesslink.gov.uk, then click on Sales and Marketing, Selling and the Law and finally The Sale of Goods Act.

Other liabilities you should consider taking insurance cover against are:

- ✓ **Public liability:** This is a legal liability to pay damages for bodily injury, illness or disease contracted by any other person, other than employees, or loss of or damage to their property caused by the insured.

- ✓ **Professional indemnity:** This provides protection against any legal action by clients who believe they received bad or negligent services, and incurred a loss as a result. Most professional companies have professional indemnity cover – in some industries it's compulsory. Anyone who supplies advice or services such as consultancy should consider professional indemnity insurance.

Finding and Choosing Business Advisers

You need lots of help to get started in business and even more when you're successful – and this help can come from accountants, banks, lawyers and management consultants, as well as possibly tax consultants, advertising and public relations consultants, technology and IT advisers, and so on. The rules and tips in the following sections should steer you through dealing with most situations involving choosing and using outside advisers.

Tallying up an accountant

Keeping your financial affairs in good order is the key to staying legal and winning any disputes. A good accountant inside or outside your company can keep you on track. A bad accountant is in the ideal position to defraud you at worst, or to derail you through negligence or incompetence.

What attributes should you look for and how can you find the right accountant for your business? The key steps to choosing a good accountant are:

- ✓ Check that the accountant is a member of one of the recognised accounting bodies such as the Chartered

Institute of Management Accountants (www.cimaglobal.com) or the Institute of Chartered Accountants in England and Wales (www.icaew.co.uk).

✔ Have a clear idea of what services you require. You need to consider how complete your bookkeeping records are likely to be, whether you need your VAT returns completed or budgets and cash-flow forecasts prepared and updated, as well as whether you require an annual audit.

✔ Clarify the charges scale at the outset. Spending a little more on bookkeeping, both staff and systems, may make more sense than leaving it all to a much higher-charging qualified accountant.

✔ Use personal recommendations from respected fellow businesspeople, particularly fellow clients of the accountant you're considering. Pay rather less attention to the recommendation of bankers, government agencies or family and friends, without totally ignoring their advice.

✔ Take references from the accountant's clients as well as from the person who recommended the accountant. They may just get on well – they may even be related!

✔ Find out what back-up the accountant has for both systems and people. The tax authorities aren't very sympathetic if you're late with your records, whatever the reason. It would be doubly annoying to be fined for someone else's tardiness.

✔ See at least three accountants before making your choice, ensuring that they deal with companies your size and a bit bigger – not so much bigger that they have no relevant advice and help to offer, but big enough for you to have some room for growth without having to change accountants too quickly.

✔ Find out which other companies the accountant acts for. You don't want the accountant to be so busy she can't service your needs properly, or to be working for potential competitors.

✔ Make the accounting appointment for a trial period only, and set a specific task to see how the accountant gets on.

✔ Give the accountant the latest accounts of your business and ask for her comments based on her analysis of the figures. You can quickly see whether she's grasped the basics of your financial position.

Investing in a bank

You may wonder why I list selecting a bank in a section covering choosing business advisers. The answer, crazy as it may seem, is that your banker is almost invariably the first person you turn to when the chips are down. You may not find this so surprising when you think about it. After all, most big business problems turn on money and bankers are the people who turn the money on.

Go for the wrong bank and you can lose more than your overdraft. You may lose the chance to acquire a free, or at least nearly free, business adviser.

The top ten questions to ask before taking on a bank manager are:

- ✔ How quickly can you make decisions about lending? Anything longer than ten days is too long.

- ✔ What rate of interest do you charge? Around 2 or 3 per cent above the Bank of England base rate is fairly normal. Above 4 per cent is on the high side.

- ✔ What factors do you take into consideration in arriving at that rate? If the bank proposes a high rate of interest, say 4 per cent above the Bank of England base rate or higher, then you need to know why. It may be that all the bank is asking for is some further security for its loan, which you may think worth giving in return for a lower interest rate.

- ✔ What other charges are there? For example, does the bank charge for every transaction in and out of an account and if so how much?

- ✔ Do you visit your clients and get to know their business? If the bank doesn't visit, how can it ever get to understand your business in depth?

- ✔ Under what circumstances does the bank want a personal guarantee? When the bank is feeling exposed to greater risk than it wants to take, it may ask you to shoulder some of that risk personally. Under the terms of a bank's loan to your business, it may state that its lending shouldn't exceed a certain sum. You need to be clear what that sum is.

✔ What help and advisory services do you have that may be useful to me? Banks often provide advice on export trade, currency dealing, insurance and a range of other related services.

✔ What's unique about your banking services that may make me want to use you rather than any other bank? This factor rather depends on what you consider to be valuable. A bank that delivers all its services on the Internet may be attractive to one person and anathema and a turnoff to another.

✔ How long may it be before my present manager moves on? If the bank routinely moves managers every few years, forming personal relationships may not be particularly valuable.

✔ Do any situations exist when you're likely to ask for early repayment of a loan? A bank may insist that if you break any major condition of the loan, such as the overdraft limit or repayment schedule, the whole loan is repayable. You need to find out whether this is so, and what sum or event may cause this to happen.

Soliciting for a lawyer

Lawyers or solicitors are people you hope never to have to use and when you do need one you need her yesterday. Even if you don't appoint a company lawyer, you may well require one for basic stuff if you're forming a company or setting up a partnership agreement. Follow the same rules as you do for choosing an accountant (refer to 'Tallying up an accountant', earlier in this chapter).

When things do go wrong, the time and money required to put them right can be an unexpected and unwelcome drain. By doing things right from the start, you can avoid at least some of the most common disputes and cope more easily with catastrophes.

In addition to ensuring that contracts are correctly drawn up, that leases are free from nasty surprises and that you're following the right health and safety procedures, a solicitor can also advise on choosing the best structure for your company, on protecting your intellectual property and on how to go about raising money.

Finding a lawyer for your business

Lawyers For Your Business (www.lawsociety.org.uk; select Find a Solicitor and then Lawyers For Your Business) represents some 1,400 firms of solicitors in England and Wales that have come together to help ensure that all businesses, especially the smaller owner-managed ones, get access to sound legal advice whenever they need it.

To remove the risk of incurring unexpectedly high legal costs, all Lawyers For Your Business members offer a free consultation, lasting at least half an hour, to diagnose your legal problem and any need for action, with full information, in advance, on the likely costs of proceeding.

The Law Society (www.lawsociety.org.uk) can send you a list of Lawyers For Your Business members in your area, and a voucher for a free consultation. Simply choose one of the firms in the list and arrange an appointment, mentioning Lawyers For Your Business and the voucher.

If you're going to see a lawyer, it's always best to be well prepared. Have all the facts to hand and know what you want help with.

Managing a consultant

If you're facing a new major problem in which you have no expertise, particularly a problem you don't expect to experience again, then hiring a consultant is an option worth considering. For example, if you're moving premises, changing your computing or accounting system, starting to do business overseas or designing an employee share ownership scheme, getting the help of someone who's covered that area several times before and who's an expert in the field may well make sense.

The time a consultant takes to carry out most tasks a small business may require is likely to be between a fortnight and three months. Anything much longer is too expensive for most small firms and anything much shorter is unlikely to have much of an impact on the business. Costs vary depending on both the skill of the consultant and the topic covered. A tax consultant, for example, can cost upwards of £450 an hour, and a training consultant may cost the same sum for a day.

Take time to brief the consultant thoroughly. Don't expect just to dump the problem on the consultant's doorstep and walk away. Set the consultant a small, measurable part of the task first and see how she performs. Never give the consultant a long-term contract or an open-ended commitment.

The Institute of Business Consulting (`www.ibconsulting.org.uk`) provides guidelines for choosing a consultant in the Purchasing Consultancy section of its website. You may also find that your local Business Link has a register of approved (and insured) specialist consultants for most business needs (find more information at `www.businesslink.gov.uk`).

Chapter 12

Keeping Track of Finances

. . . .

In This Chapter

▶ Keeping essential records

▶ Understanding the main accounting reports

▶ Analysing financial data

▶ Meeting profit goals

▶ Evaluating financial performance

▶ Staying on the right side of the law

. . . .

*E*very business needs reliable financial information for both decision making and accountability. No one is going to be keen to pump money into your venture if you can't demonstrate that you know what's likely to happen to it. Reliable information doesn't necessarily call for complex bookkeeping and accounting systems: simple is often best. As the business grows, and perhaps takes on outside investors, you require more sophisticated information. That's when using a computer and some of the relevant software packages may be the best way forward. But even with a computer errors can occur, so you have to know how to recognise when financial information goes wrong and how you can correct it.

You have a legal obligation in business to keep accounting records from the outset and not just wait until your business runs into serious problems. If as a director or owner of a business you can't see when you're heading for a financial reef, you may find yourself in deep trouble, if not actually heading for jail – and definitely not collecting £200 on the way.

Keeping the Books

To survive and prosper in business you need to know how much cash you have, and what your profit or loss on sales is. You need these facts on at least a monthly, weekly or occasionally even a daily basis to survive, let alone grow.

Recording financial information

Although bad luck plays a part in some business failures, a lack of reliable financial information plays a part in most. However, businesses have all the information they need to manage well close at hand. Among the bills you have to pay, invoices to raise, petty cash slips to file and bank statements to diagnose, you have enough to give you a true picture of your business's performance.

All you need to do is record and organise that information so that the financial picture becomes clear. The way you record financial information is called *bookkeeping*.

Not only the business owner needs these financial facts. Bankers, shareholders and tax inspectors are unsympathetic audiences to anyone without well-documented facts to back them up. If, for example, a tax authority presents a business with a tax demand, the onus then lies with the businessperson, using his records, either to agree or dispute the sum claimed.

In any event, if you plan to trade as a limited company, the Companies Act 1985 requires you 'to keep adequate records sufficient to show and explain the company's transactions'.

Reasons for keeping proper records:

- ✔ To know the cash position of your business precisely and accurately

- ✔ To discover how profitable your business really is

- ✔ To see which of your activities are profitable and which aren't

- ✔ To give bankers and other sources of finance confidence that your business is being well managed and that their money is in good hands

 ✔ To allow you to calculate your tax bill accurately

 ✔ To help you prepare timely financial forecasts and projections

 ✔ To make sure that you both collect and pay money due correctly

 ✔ To keep accountancy and audit costs to a minimum

Starting simple with single entry

If you're doing books by hand and don't have a lot of transactions, the single-entry method is the easiest acceptable way to go.

Single entry means that you write down each transaction in your records once, preferably on a ledger sheet. You record the flow of income and expenses through your business by making a running total of money taken in (gross receipts) and money paid out (payments or, as they're sometimes called, *disbursements*). You should keep receipts and payments and summarise them daily, weekly or monthly, as the business needs require. At the end of the year, you total up the 12 monthly summaries. You're ready for tax time.

You may benefit from separating different types of income and expense into categories, for example stock, vehicles, telephone, as in Figure 12-1. This lets you see how much you're spending or receiving in each area.

Payments				Analysis			
Date	Name	Details	Amount £	Stocks	Vehicles	Telephone	Other
4 June	Gibbs	Stock purchase	310	310			
8 June	Gibbs	Stock purchase	130	130			
12 June	ABC Telecoms	Telephone charges	55.23			55.23	
18 June	Colt Rentals	Vehicle hire	87.26		87.26		
22 June	VV Mobiles	Mobile phone	53.24			53.24	
27 June	Gibbs	Stock purchase	36.28	36.28			
Totals			672.01	476.28	87.26	108.47	

Figure 12-1: An example of an analysed cash book.

You need to keep copies of paid and unpaid sales invoices and the same for purchases, as well as your bank statements. You then 'reconcile' (match) bank statements to your cash book to tie everything together.

If you're taking credit from suppliers or giving credit to customers, then you need to keep information on such matters as how long the money has been owed and what interest penalties, if any, will be applied to late payments, as well as the cash book, whether you analyse it or not.

Dealing with double entry

If you operate a partnership or trade as a company, then you may need a double-entry bookkeeping system from the start.

A *double-entry bookkeeping system* requires two entries for each transaction – hence the name – and every transaction has two effects on the accounts. For example, when you buy an item of stock for sale and pay for it in cash, your cash balance goes down and your amount of stock goes up by the same amount, keeping everything in balance.

Choosing the right accounting program

With the cost of a basic computerised accounting system starting at barely £50, and a reasonable package costing between £200 and £500, planning to use such a system from the outset is sensible. If you're at all concerned as to whether such software represents value try out Intuits SimpleStart (`http://quickbooks.intuit.co.uk`). It's completely free for ever. The only catch is that although it's a fully functioning accounting package, you're limited to just 20 customers and suppliers.With a computer you have no more arithmetical errors. As long as you enter the information correctly, the computer adds it up correctly. With a computer, the £53.24 mobile phone expenditure in Figure 12-1 is input as an expense (a debit), and then the computer automatically posts it to the mobile phone account as a credit. In effect, the computer eliminates the extra step or the need to master the difference between debit and credit.

A computerised accounting program is only as good as the data you enter into it. Introduce strict end-of-month controls to make sure that you've counted and valued all stock, that you've dealt with all the month's invoices and so on. Without this, your computer program reflects inaccurate data.

Routine tasks, such as filling in tax and value added tax (VAT) returns, take minutes rather than days with a computer. The system can ensure that your returns are accurate and fully reconciled. With a computerised system, invoices are always accurate. You can see at a glance which customers regularly take too long to pay.

You have two main options in your choice of your first accounting system. If you think that a manual system is best for your purposes, you can get sheets of analysis paper with printed columns for accounting entries, and put in your own headings as appropriate. Or you can buy off-the-shelf manual sets of books from any office stationer's outlet. These cost anything from £10 to £20 for a full set of ledgers. Hingston Publishing (www.hingston-publishing.co.uk) produces small business accounts systems for both VAT and non-VAT registered businesses for about £15.

If you decide to take the plunge and go straight for accounting software, then you have a myriad of software providers to choose from that serve the small business market with software for bookkeeping. These are some of the more popular packages:

- ✔ MYOB (Mind Your Own Business; www.mamut.com/uk/myob) offers a range of bookkeeping systems starting with its Mamut Office Mini licensed out at £59 per annum and going up to Mamut Enterprise E5, costing £408 per annum.

- ✔ TAS Books Small Business Edition (SBE; www.tas software.co.uk) is aimed specifically at the needs of new, smaller companies. Online support within the product is generally comprehensive, and a manual helps to explain more advanced features. It offers a basic system for free and then a range of more sophisticated ones on yearly subscriptions from around a £100.

- ✔ QuickBooks (www.intuit.co.uk) offers a range of products from £99 to £499. The most sophisticated of its products has budgeting, forecasting and an advanced reporting too where you can choose from over 135 templates, or build your own advanced reports.)

- ✔ Sage's (http://shop.sage.co.uk/accountssoftware.aspx) entry product Sage Instant Accounts v16, which comes in at about £135, bears reasonable comparison with some of the other products on the market. Sage 50 Accounts 2011 is a heavy-duty program weighing in at a correspondingly hefty £650.

Outsourcing bookkeeping

Accountants and freelance bookkeepers can do all your book-keeping work – at a price. The rate is anything from £20 per hour upwards.

Bookkeeping services range from a basic write-up of the entries and leave-the-rest-to-you approach, through to providing weekly or monthly accounts, perhaps with pointers as to what may be going wrong. Services even exist that act as a virtual finance director, giving you access to a senior accountant who may sit on your board.

Most bookkeeping services have a computer system into which you have to plug your records, so if you're thinking of going down this route check out which software you require first.

The bookkeeper's most routine but vital task may be doing the payroll. If you don't get this done on time and correctly, both staff and HM Revenue and Customs, for which you have to collect pay as you earn (PAYE), becomes restless. A weekly payroll service for up to ten employees costs upwards of £85 per month. If you pay everyone monthly, the cost drops to about a third of that figure.

If you go down this route you probably need someone local, so ask around to find someone who uses a bookkeeper and is satisfied. Alternatively, turn to the phone book.

As with an accountant, make sure that a prospective book-keeper is adequately qualified. The International Association of Book-keepers (IAB; website www.iab.org.uk; tel. 01732 458080) and the Association of Certified Bookkeepers (ACB; tel. 0208 749 7126) are the two professional associations concerned.

You can check out the letters that anyone in the accounting profession uses after his name or the bodies he claims to be a member of at the Directory of Essential Accountancy Abbreviations, which the Library and Information Service at the Institute of Chartered Accountants in England and Wales maintains (`www.icaew.com`; go to Library and then A–Z).

Understanding Your Accounts

Keeping the books is one thing, but being able to make good use of the information those accounts contain is quite another. You need to turn the raw accounting data from columns of figures into statements of account. Those accounts in turn tell you how much cash your business has, its profit or loss numbers and how much money you have tied up in the business to produce those results. The following sections discuss some of the key accounting statements and performance analyses.

Forecasting Cash Flow

In the language of accounting, income is recognised when a product or service has been sold, delivered or executed, and the invoice raised. Although that rule holds good for calculating profit (see 'Reporting Your Profits', later in this chapter), it doesn't apply when forecasting cash flow.

Profit is what may be generated if all goes well and customers pay up, and you can think of cash flow as the cold shower of reality, bringing you sharply back to your senses.

 Overtrading describes a business that's expanding beyond its financial resources. As sales expand, the amount of cash tied up in stocks and customers' credit grows rapidly. Pressure also comes from suppliers of goods and services and from additional employees, who all expect to be paid. The natural escape valve for pressures on working capital is an overdraft (or a substantial increase in the existing one). Monitoring cash flow reduces the risk of overtrading.

Reporting Your Profits

A key use of bookkeeping information is to prepare a profit and loss account.

In carrying out any business activity, two very different actions go on. One is selling your goods and services and getting paid for them. Money comes in – perhaps not immediately, but it usually shows up eventually. This money goes by a variety of names, including *revenues*, *income* and *sales income*. The second transaction is the outlay you make in order to provide the goods and services you sell to your customers. Some of the costs you incur are for raw materials, salaries, rents and so forth. These costs are known as *expenses*. By deducting your expenses from your income, you end up with the profit (or loss) for the particular period under review.

At its simplest, the profit and loss account has at its head the period covered, followed by the income, from which you deduct all the expenses of the business to arrive at the profit (or loss) made in the period. Figure 12-2 shows a sample account.

Profit and Loss Account for Year to 31 March 201X	£
Income	1,416,071
Less expenses	1,389,698
Profit	26,373

Figure 12-2: A basic profit and loss account.

Although the information shown in the profit and loss account is certainly better than nothing, you can use basic bookkeeping information to give you a much richer picture of events within the business. Provided, that is, that you've set up the right analysis headings in the first place.

The following sections show, step by step, how to build up a profit and loss account to give you a more complete picture of the trading events of the past year at Safari Europe, the example I use in the following sections.

Calculating gross profit

One of the most important figures in the profit and loss account is the gross profit. Whatever your activity, you have to buy certain 'raw materials'. Those include anything you have to buy to produce the goods and services you're selling. So if you sell cars, the cost of buying in the cars is a raw materials cost. In Safari's case, because the company is in the travel business, the costs of airline tickets and hotel rooms are the raw material of a package holiday.

The amount left from the sales revenues after deducting the cost of sales, as these costs of 'making' are known, is the *gross profit*. This is really the only discretionary money coming into the business, where you have some say over how it's spent. Figure 12-3 shows a sample profit calculation.

Safari Europe
Profit and Loss Account for year to   31 March 201X

Income

Tours sold	1,402,500
Insurance & other services	13,571
Non-operating revenue	0
Total income	1,416,071

Less **Cost of goods sold**

Tours bought	1,251,052
Insurance & other services	4,071
Total cost of goods sold	1,255,123
Gross profit	160,948

Figure 12-3: An example of gross profit calculation.

In the account shown in Figure 12-3 you can see that Safari has two sources of income, one from tours and one from insurance and other related services. It also, of course, has the costs associated with buying in holidays and insurance policies from suppliers.

The difference between the income of £1,416,071 and the cost of the 'goods' the company has sold is just £160,948. That's the sum that the management has to run the business, not the much larger headline-making figure of nearly £1.5 million.

Figure 12-4 shows how to calculate gross profit in a business that makes things rather than selling services.

	£
Sales	100,000
Cost of goods sold	65,000
Gross profit	35,000

Figure 12-4: A manufacturer's gross profit.

In the example in Figure 12-4, the basic sum is the same as for a service business, as shown in Figure 12-3. Take the cost of goods from the sales income and what's left is gross profit. However, a business that makes things holds raw materials, and you only want to count in the cost of goods sold the materials actually used. You do this by noting the stock at the start of the period, adding in any purchases made and deducting the closing stock.

You also need to build in the labour cost in production and any overheads, such as workshop usage, and deduct those in order to arrive at the gross profit, as shown in Figure 12-5.

	£	£	£
Sales			**100,000**
Manufacturing costs			
Raw materials opening stock	30,000		
Purchases in period	25,000		
	55,000		
Less Raw materials closing stock	15,500		
Cost of materials used		39,500	
Direct labour cost		18,000	
Manufacturing overhead cost			
Indirect labour	4,000		
Workshop heat, light and power	3,500		
Total manufacturing costs		7,500	
Cost of goods sold			65,000
Gross profit			35,000

Figure 12-5: Expanded gross profit calculation.

Reckoning expenses

After you calculate the gross profit, you have to allow for all the expenses that are likely to arise in running the business. Using the Safari case as a working example, Figure 12-6 shows all the costs usually associated with running the business, such as rent, rates, telephone, marketing and promotion, and so forth. Although all these expenses are correctly included, they aren't all allowable for tax purposes in all countries.

Safari Europe

Profit and Loss Account for
the year to 31 March 201X

	Year 1
Income	
Tours sold	1,402,500
Insurance & other services	13,571
Non-operating revenue	0
Total income	1,416,071
Less **Cost of goods sold**	
Tours bought	1,251,052
Insurance & other services	4,071
Total cost of goods sold	1,255,123
Gross profit	160,948
Expenditure	
Rent & rates	18,000
Heat, light & power	3,500
Telephone system lease	2,000
Computer leasing	5,000
Marketing & promotion	12,500
Postage & stationery	3,250
Telephone	3,575
Insurance & legal	3,500
Wages (not owner's)	36,000
Consultancy services	25,000
Membership & subscription	1,500
Travel & subsistence	4,250
Training & staff development	6,000
Depreciation of fixtures	5,500
Total expenditure	129,575

Figure 12-6: Business expenses.

The Total expenditure heading isn't quite accurate. Other expenses associated with running a business aren't included here, but these expenses are treated in a slightly different way, for reasons that will become apparent as you read on about the different types of profit.

Appreciating the different types of profit

You can measure profit in several ways:

✓ **Gross profit** is the profit left after you've deducted all costs related to making what you sell from income (see the beginning of this section, 'Reporting Your Profits', for what represents income).

✓ **Operating profit** is what's left after you take the expenses (or expenditure) away from the gross profit.

✓ **Profit before tax** is what you get after deducting any financing costs. This is a measure of the performance of the management, which is important if the owners and managers aren't the same people, as may be the case when you start to employ staff. The reasoning here is that the operating management can have little influence over the way in which the business is financed (no borrowings means no interest expenses, for example), or the level of interest charges.

Interestingly enough, when it comes to valuing the business, the operating profit is generally used as the multiplying factor (so many times earnings is a typical valuation mechanism and operating profit is used to represent earnings).

Taking away the financing costs, in the example £5,000 interest charges, leaves a profit before tax of £26,373, as shown in Figure 12-7. Finally, you deduct tax to leave the net profit after tax, the bottom line. This sum belongs to the owners of the business and, if it's a limited company, is what dividends can be paid from.

Safari Europe

Profit and Loss Account for the year to 31 March 201X	
Income	
Tours sold	1,402,500
Insurance & other services	13,571
Non-operating revenue	0
Total income	1,416,071
Less **Cost of goods sold**	
Tours bought	1,251,052
Insurance & other services	4,071
Total cost of goods sold	1,255,123
Gross profit	160,948
Expenditure	
Rent & rates	18,000
Heat, light & power	3,500
Telephone system lease	2,000
Computer leasing	5,000
Marketing & promotion	12,500
Postage & stationery	3,250
Telephone	3,575
Insurance & legal	3,500
Wages (not owner's)	36,000
Consultancy services	25,000
Membership & subscription	1,500
Travel & subsistence	4,250
Training & staff development	6,000
Depreciation of fixtures	5,500
Total expenditure	129,575
Operating profit	31,373
Less interest charges	5,000
Net profit before tax	26,373
Tax	5,538
Net profit after tax	20,835

Figure 12-7: Levels of profit.

Accounting for Pricing

Setting a selling price for your wares is one of the most important and most frequent business decisions that anyone running a business has to make. At first glance it doesn't seem such a big deal. Just add up all the costs, add a healthy profit margin and as long as the customers don't rush for the exit you're in business. Unfortunately, the first part of that sentence contains a few traps for the unwary.

Complications start when you have to get to grips with the characteristics of costs. Not all costs behave in exactly the same way. For example, the rent on a shop, office or workshop is a fixed sum, payable monthly or quarterly. Your landlord doesn't usually expect you to pay more rent if you get more customers, nor is he especially generous if you have a particularly lean period. The business rates on any premises and the cost of an advertisement in the local paper are also *fixed costs*. That term shows that the cost in question doesn't vary directly with the volume of sales, not that the cost itself has been immutably settled and you're committed to pay it. You don't have to advertise and you do have to pay business rates, but both are fixed costs.

Contrast that with the cost of the products you plan to sell. Assume for a moment that you're selling just one product, a bottle of wine costing £3 to buy in. The more you sell, the more your stock costs to buy. That type of cost varies directly with the volume of sales you achieve, and in a rare display of user-friendliness from the accounting profession is known as *variable*. The cost of each individual bottle may or may not vary – your supplier may or may not change the price, perhaps lowering it to win more business from you or upping it to meet the chancellor of the exchequer's ever-growing demand for more tax. But the nature of the cost means that the total cost does vary as your sales volume changes.

Breaking even

To keep things simple: your business plans to sell only one product, the wine I mention in the previous text, and you only have one fixed cost, the rent. Figure 12-8 sets out a graphical picture of how your costs stack up. The vertical axis shows the value of sales and costs in £'000s and the horizontal axis the number of units sold, in this case bottles of wine. The rent is £10,000 for the year, represented by a straight line labelled 'fixed costs'. The angled line running from the top of the fixed costs line shows the amount of the variable costs. Sell zero bottles and you incur zero additional costs. In this case the total costs are £10,000 plus £0 = £10,000. Every bottle you buy in adds £3 of variable costs (you have to buy the wine in!!) to the total costs.

You need to calculate the break-even point – that is, when you've made enough money from selling wine to pay the rent. The sales revenue line moves up at an angle from the bottom left-hand corner of the graph. If you plan to sell your wine at £5 a bottle, you calculate the figures for this line by multiplying the number of units sold by that price.

The break-even point is the stage at which a business starts to make a profit – when the money coming in from sales is higher than the fixed and variable costs added together. For your wine business, you can see from the chart that this point arises when you've sold 5,000 bottles. You don't have to draw a chart every time you want to work out your break-even point – you can use a simple formula.

Break-even point = Fixed costs

Selling price – Unit variable cost

$$= \quad \frac{10,000}{5-3} = 5,000 \text{ units}$$

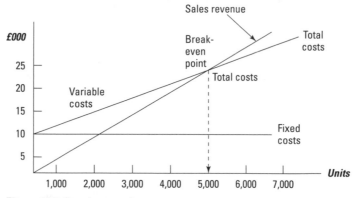

Figure 12-8: Break-even chart.

Building in more products

The example so far has been for a one-product company, but what if you plan to sell more than just one type of wine – or perhaps even add crisps and chocolates too? When you reach this stage you need to work from your gross profit percentage.

If, for example, you're aiming for a 40 per cent gross profit, your fixed costs are £10,000 and your profit goal is £4,000, then the sum is as follows:

$$BEPP = \frac{10,000 + 4,000}{0.4} = \frac{14,000}{0.4} = £35,000$$

If you got a bit lost about where the 0.4 came from, don't worry; that's just 40 per cent expressed as a decimal, a step you need to take before you can use the number. What you now know is that at a 40 per cent gross profit margin you need to sell £35,000 worth of wine, chocolates and crisps to hit your profit goal. Your accountant can help with these calculations, and the Harvard Business School website has a useful tutorial that links with its break-even spreadsheet.

Harvard Business School offers a free downloadable interactive break-even workbook (`http://hbswk.hbs.edu/archive/1262.html`), one of several workbooks/tutorials from the HBS Toolkit used by its students.

Balancing the Books

You have to know where you are now before making any plans to go anywhere else. Without a starting point any journey is bound to be a confusing experience. A business sums up its current position in a balance sheet, the business's primary reporting document. The balance sheet contains the cumulative evidence of financial events, showing where money has come from and what's been done with that money. Logically, the two sums must balance.

In practical terms, balancing your sums takes quite a bit of work, not the least of which isn't necessarily the balancing part, but figuring out the numbers. Your cash-in-hand figure is probably dead right, but can you say the same of the value of your assets? Accountants have their own rules on how to arrive at these figures, but they don't pretend to be anything more than an approximation. Every measuring device has inherent inaccuracies, and financial controls are no exception.

A balance sheet

In formal accounts the figures are set out vertically rather than in horizontal fashion, reflected in Figure 12-9. The business's long-term borrowings, in this case the mortgage and hire purchase charges, are named *Creditors, amounts falling due in over 1 year* and deducted from the total assets to show the *Net total assets* being employed.

The bottom of the balance sheet in Figure 12-9 shows how the owners of the business have supported these assets, in this case by their own funds. As you can see later, they could also have invested profit made in earlier years back into the business (see the later section 'Understanding reserves'). I've also assumed that the owner's house is now a business premises owned by her company. (This assumption has wider implications, but none that's relevant to the arithmetic or the balance sheet.)

Categorising assets

Accountants describe *assets* as valuable resources, owned by a business, which were acquired at a measurable monetary cost.

The exception to the *paid for* part is the grey area of goodwill. *Goodwill* is the value placed on the business's reputation and other intangible assets – a brand name, for example. Assessing the value of this asset is of particular interest to those buying or selling a business.

One useful convention recommends listing assets in the balance sheet in their order of permanence; that is, starting out with the most difficult to turn into cash and working down to cash itself. This structure is very practical when you're looking at someone else's balance sheet, or comparing balance sheets. It can also help you to recognise obvious information gaps quickly.

	£	£
NET ASSETS EMPLOYED		
Fixed assets		
Premises	150,000	
Car	7,000	
Furniture	1500	
Jewellery and paintings	350	
Book value		158,850
Current assets		
Money owed by sister	135	
Cash	50	
Total current assets	185	
***Less* Current liabilities**		
Overdraft	100	
Credit cards	50	
Total current liabilities	150	
Net current assets		35
Total assets		158,885
Less: Creditors, amounts falling due in over 1 year		45,500
Net total assets		**113,385**
FINANCED BY		
My capital	113,385	
Total owners' funds		113,385

Figure 12-9: Jane Smith Limited Balance Sheet at 5 April, 201X.

Accounting for liabilities

Liabilities are claims against the business. These claims may include such items as tax, accruals (which are expenses for items used but not yet billed for, such as telephone and other utilities), deferred income, overdrafts, loans, hire purchase and money owed to suppliers. Liabilities can also be less easy to identify and even harder to put a figure on, bad debts being a prime example.

Understanding reserves

Reserves are the accumulated profits that a business makes over its working life, which the owner has ploughed back into the business rather than taking them out.

Jane Smith's balance sheet (see the earlier section 'A balance sheet') shows her capital as being the sole support for the liabilities of the business. The implication is that she put this whole sum in at once. In practice, this is much more likely to have happened over time, and in a variety of ways.

Perhaps she started out in business, because that is how you must now look at her affairs, with a sum of, say, £25,000. In the period since she's been in business she's made a net profit after tax of £50,000 and put this back into her business to finance growth. In addition, the premises that she bought a few years ago for £111,615 have just been revalued at £150,000, a paper gain of £38,385.

The bottom portion of her company balance sheet may now look as shown in Figure 12-10.

	£	£
FINANCED BY		
Capital introduced		25,000
Reserves		
Capital reserve	38,385	
Revenue reserve	50,000	88,385
		113,385

Figure 12-10: Jane's reserves.

The profit of £50,000 ploughed back into the business is called a *revenue reserve*, which means that the money actually exists and can be used to buy stock or more assets. The increase in value of the business premises is, on the other hand, a *paper* increase. Jane can't use the £38,385 increase in *capital reserves* to buy anything, because it's not in money form until the premises are sold. However, she can use that paper reserve to underpin a loan from the bank, so turning a paper profit into a cash resource. Both reserves and the capital introduced represent all the money that the shareholder has invested in this venture.

Keeping on the Right Side of the Law

Whether the money in the business is yours alone, provided by family and friends or supplied by outside financial institutions, you have a legal responsibility to make sure you keep your accounts in good order at all times. If you're successful and need more money to expand, you need financial information to prove your case. If things aren't going so well and you need to strengthen your position to weather a financial storm, then you have even greater need of good accounting information.

Whatever the circumstances in the background, tax and VAT authorities need to be certain that your figures are correct and timely.

Filing Your Accounts

If you're trading as a company then you have to file your accounts with Companies House (www.companieshouse. gov.uk) each year.

Unless you're filing your company's first accounts, the time normally allowed for delivering accounts to Companies House is ten months from the end of the relevant accounting period for private companies. If you're filing your company's first accounts and they cover a period of more than 12 months, you must deliver them to the registrar within 22 months of the date of incorporation for private companies. Late filing will attract financial penalties details of which you can find on the Companies House website.

Managing Your Tax Position

The government raises some £600 billion each year in one form of tax or another; that represents around 40 pence in every pound earned. Not only is the amount colossal but now about a zillion ways exist in which tax is raised. Aside from income tax, VAT (value added tax) and NI (national insurance), which most people brush across, there are taxes or reliefs from paying tax on fuel, capital gains, capital expenditure, research and development, business rates, excise duty, a climate change levy, air passenger duty, landfill tax, an aggregates levy, small company tax relief, vehicle excise duties and stamp duties, to mention but a few that the successful owner manger can expect to encounter. Each of these tax categories, in turn have a number of their own categories. VAT, for example, is levied at a standard rate, reduced rate, zero rate and exempt from VAT altogether, and the government shifts about the 50 or so product and service categories within each VAT category from time to time. The government has made 44 major changes to the tax system in the UK since 1979 and a couple of thousand minor ones.

If you think that all, or even most, of the profit you make in your business comes your way, think again. The government takes a sizeable slice of everything you make, in one way or another, and gets very nasty if you try to evade its clutches. You may be starting your first business, but government agencies have had centuries to hone their skills in extracting their pound of flesh.

Before you reach for your passport and head offshore, taxing entrepreneurs is a fact of life in almost every country in the world, though both the amounts and methods of assessment vary widely. Surprisingly enough, the tax climate in the UK is relatively benign and people here pay less than most. So although you may have to pay tax, you don't have to pay too much. As a Morgan Stanley advert succinctly puts it, 'You must pay taxes. But there's no law that says you gotta leave a tip.

Adding up income tax

Under the self-assessment tax system in the UK, you pay taxes for your accounting year in the calendar year in which that accounting year ends. Special rules apply for the first year and the last year of trading to ensure tax is charged fairly.

If your turnover is low – currently in the UK less than £15,000 per year – you can summarise your income on three lines: sales, expenses and profit. If your turnover is above the minimum, you have to summarise your accounts to show turnover, gross profit and expenses by account categories, such as vehicle running costs, advertising, telephone and rent.

No matter how you account for your business income, as a sole trader or partnership you get to deduct a personal allowance amount from your profit figure, paying income tax on your profit minus your personal allowance. The personal allowance is the current threshold below which you don't pay tax.

Looking at levies on companies

Companies have a legal identity separate from those who work in them, whether or not those workers also own the company. Everyone working in the business is taxed as an employee. The company is responsible through the pay as you earn (PAYE) system for collecting tax and passing it to the tax authorities.

Directors' salaries are a business expense, just as with any other wages, and are deducted from the company's revenues in arriving at its taxable profits.

Companies in the UK pay tax in three main ways at rates that can change each year.

- ✔ **Corporation tax** is paid on the company's profits for the year, currently 20 per cent.

- ✔ **Dividend payment taxes** are levied on the distribution of profit to shareholders.

- ✔ **Capital gains tax** is owed if a company sells an asset, say a business property, at a profit.

The current company tax rates are published on HM Revenue and Customs' website (www.hmrc.gov.uk/rates/corp.htm).

Valuing value-added tax

As well as paying tax on profits, every business over a certain size has, in effect, to collect taxes too. VAT (value added tax) is a tax on consumer spending. It's a European system, although most countries have significant variations in VAT rates, starting thresholds and the schemes themselves.

Essentially, you must register to collect VAT if your taxable turnover – that is, your sales (not profit) – exceeds £68,000 in any 12-month period (£70,000 if you sell by mail order or via the Internet) or looks as though it may reasonably be expected to do so. This rate is reviewed each year in the budget and changes frequently.

You get no reward for collecting VAT, but you are penalised for making mistakes or for sending returns in late.

HM Revenue and Customs' website (go to www.hmrc.gov.uk, select Businesses and Corporations, and then VAT) has useful information on every aspect of the subject, including details of all VAT rates and procedures.

Paying PAYE

Income tax is collected from employees through the pay as you earn (PAYE) system. The employee's liability to income tax is collected as it's earned instead of by tax assessment at a later date. If the business is run as a limited company, then the directors of the company are employees. PAYE must be operated on all salaries and bonuses paid to directors, your-self included.

HM Revenue and Customs now issues booklets in reasonably plain English about how PAYE works and have extensive help on their website (www.hmrc.gov.uk/paye/index.htm).

Calculating National Insurance

National Insurance is paid by employers and employees. For owner managers you calculate national insurance is based on taxable profits. The percentage you pay depends on what range your profits fall in. Expect to pay around 8 per cent if the number falls in a range from approximately £5,000 to £44,000. Above that figure, you pay 1 per cent. This is paid in addition to the flat-rate Class 2 national insurance contribu-tions of about £2.40 per week.

All these rates and amounts change in March of every year, but the broad principles remain the same. You can find the latest national insurance contribution rates on HM Revenue and Customs' website (www.hmrc.gov.uk/rates/nic.htm).

Tax Cafe (www.taxcafe.co.uk) publishes a range of regularly updated tax advice guides aimed at anyone wanting to find out how to pay less tax legally. It also offers an online tax advice service, where you can ask experts complex business tax questions, including those on VAT. Responses in three to five working days cost £89.95. The Express service, where questions asked before 12 noon on a working day are answered the same day, costs £129.95. Anyone using either of these services also receives a complimentary electronic copy of their comprehensive tax guide *How to Save Tax*, worth £19.95.

Chapter 13

Doing Business Online

● ●

In This Chapter

▶ Understanding the power of the Internet and how to use it

▶ Checking out how you can add value to your business online

▶ Getting help with your website

▶ Making sure you get seen online

▶ Tracking traffic

● ●

Sure no one has yet sold a battleship online, though I guess if it was possible the government would have at least one aircraft carrier to put on its website. Hard to see how it would fit into a "shopping basket". Nevertheless according to AM Online (www.am-online.com/NewCarSalesFigures), an automotive media publication, in August 2010 some 55, 305 new motor vehicles were sold online, including 25 Bentleys, 275 Jaguars and 125 Porches. According to the Office for National Statistics (www.statistics.gov.uk/pdfdir/rs1010.pdf) the average weekly value of Internet retail sales in the UK in September 2010 was £481 million, which equated to approximately 8.8 per cent of total retail sales.

A report commissioned by Google, published in October 2010 indicated that Britons spend a higher proportion of their money online than any other country in the Organisation of Economic Co-operation and Development (OECD), another name for the world's richest countries. Hardly surprising then to conclude that no self respecting entrepreneur will stay in business for long without some form of online presence.

Appreciating the Power of the Internet

So just how big is the Internet? Well, in September 2010, when I was writing this edition, over 2 billion people, more than a quarter of the world's population, were online and using methods of connectivity infinitely superior to the early primitive telephone links. That growth has itself been overtaken by the volume of traffic driven over the Internet itself. According to industry estimates some 150 exabytes (billion gigabytes) of data washed through the Internet in 2005. By 2010 that had risen to 1,200 exabytes, a growth of 700 per cent.

Clicks and bricks

Of course the Internet business world and the 'real' world overlap and, in some cases, overtake. Woolworths, for example, died on the UK high street in 2009 only to be born again on the Internet. Many of the old economy entrants to the e-economy have kept the 'mortar' as well as acquiring 'clicks'. Trust stems from customers being able to physically see what the company stands for. Tesco, a UK-based international retailer, uses specially developed software to offer an intelligent Internet tool that reacts to customers' shopping habits, suggesting different sites related to subjects or products they're interested in. In that way Tesco hopes to build a similar level of trust to that achieved in its stores, but over the Internet. The firm uses its local stores for 'pick and pack' and delivers locally using smaller vehicles.

Recognising the limits – there are none!

Even if you think that e-business offers you few advantages you could find yourself facing a range of unexpected threats and competitors heading your way courtesy of the Internet. For example, the competitors that a new offline business currently faces are probably small and perhaps even big firms in its own country or area and large international firms from elsewhere in the world. But with the Internet the new business could now have small firms similar to itself, but based anywhere in the world, entering its market. Potentially, this could put the business starter up against hundreds if not thousands of competitors, all with the advantages of nimbleness and being driven by hungry entrepreneurs just like the business starter – you too, of course.

What You Can Do Online

You could be forgiven for thinking that a website is just for those who plan to sell on the Internet. That's certainly a powerful argument for getting online and perhaps the easiest one to justify financially. Using a website to sell is so important that I've given that topic a whole section to itself in this chapter (see 'Selling Goods and Services'). But selling isn't the only valuable use your business can get from being on the Internet.

Generating advertising revenue

When you have a website you have 'readers' who other people will pay to reach, just as they would if you had a hard copy magazine. You can sell space on your website yourself, but you should be too busy running your business to get diverted with this type of distraction. The easiest way to get advertising revenue is to get someone else to do the hard work. Google Adsense (www.google.co.uk/adsense), for example, matches advertisements to your site's content and you earn money every time someone clicks an ad on your site.

You can check out the dozens of other affiliate advertising schemes at Internet Ad Sales (www.internetadsales.com), a site that reviews all online advertising products and trends.

Recruiting staff

When you start to grow your business you can advertise for staff on your own website. In that way you can be sure applicants know something of your business and you could cut out most of the costs of recruitment.

Nearly a quarter of all jobs are filled using *job boards*, websites where employees and employers can get together much along the lines of a dating agency. The Internet's advantages are speed, cost and reach. You can get your job offer in front of thousands of candidates in seconds. The fees are usually modest, often less than regional paper job adverts. Services through job boards range from passive were employers and employees just find each other, to the proactive where the website searches online candidate databases and makes suitable candidates aware of your vacancy. Useful sites include:

- **Futurestep** (`www.futurestep.com`): Covers all job functions and industry sectors.

- **Monster** (`www.monster.co.uk`): Attracts approximately 100,000 visits per month and contains over a million curricula vitae. Its vacancies cover every industry sector and regional area.

- **Webrecruit** (`www.webrecruit.co.uk`): Though the fee is a relatively high £595, they'll reimburse you if they can't fill your job.

Answering frequent questions

Businesses get dozens of phone calls and letters asking essentially the same questions. By having an Frequently Asked Questions (FAQ) section on your website you can head off most of those enquiries and save time and money.

Vebtools (`http://vebtools.com/faqs-generator`) have a free FAQ generator. Just enter the questions you receive frequently and their respective answers, click the generate button and the script outputs a complete FAQ page for you.

Carrying out research

The Internet is a rich source of market data, much of it free and immediately available. But you can't always be certain that the information is reliable or free of bias because it can be difficult if not impossible to always work out who exactly is providing the information. That being said, you can get some valuable pointers as to whether or not what you plan to sell has a market, how big that market is and who else trades in that space. The following sources should be your starting point:

✔ **Google Trends** (`www.google.co.uk/trends`) provides a snapshot on what the world is most interested in at any one moment. For example, if you're thinking of starting a bookkeeping service, entering that into the search pane produces a snazzy graph showing how interest measured by the number of searches is growing (or contracting) since January 2004 when Google started collecting the data. You can also see that South Africa has the greatest interest and the Netherlands the lowest. You can tweak the graph to show seasonality thus showing that Croydon registers the greatest interest in the UK overall and 'demand' peaks in September and bottoms out in November.

✔ **Google News** (`http://news.google.co.uk`) contains links to any newspaper article anywhere in the world covering a particular topic over the last decade or so listed by year. Asking for information on baby clothes, for example, reveals recent articles on how much the average family spends on baby clothes, the launch of a thrift store specialising in second-hand baby clothes and the launch of an organic baby clothes catalogue.

✔ **Microsoft** (`http://adlab.microsoft.com/ Demographics-Prediction`) is testing a product that can give you masses of data on market demographics (age, sex, income), purchase intentions and a search funnel tool that helps you understand how your market searches the Internet. Using the demographics tool you can find that 76 per cent of people showing an interest in baby clothes are female and, surprisingly, 24 per cent are male. The peak age group is the 25- to 34-year-olds and the lowest is the under 18s, followed by the over 50s.

✔ **Blogs** are sites where people, informed and ignorant, converse about a particular topic. The information on blogs is more straw in the wind that fact. Globe of Blogs (`www.globeofblogs.com`), launched in 2002, claims to be the first comprehensive world weblog directory. It links up to some 70,000 blogs, searchable by country, topic and about any other criteria you care to name. Google (`http://blogsearch.google.com`) is also a search engine to the world's blogs.

By running surveys online you can find out more about your customers' needs, check out whether new products or services would appeal to them and monitor complaints, so preventing them becoming problems. Zoomerang (www.zoomerang.com) and Instant Survey (www.instantsurvey.com) are among a host of companies providing free or nearly free online survey tools.

Establishing an Internet Presence

Thousands of small companies seduced into having a presence on the web quickly become disappointed. Part of the reason is that in the rush to put together a website they end up with little more than an online leaflet or brochure. *E-commerce*, which is where the real value from being on the Internet arises, only comes about when you can buy and sell products and services, just as you can with any other route to market, and equally importantly when you can open up a dialogue with customers. That conversation can be as simple as a strong FAQ section, a blog or an invitation to ask for specific information.

It's worth persevering because the gain is almost always worth the pain. Some of the other benefits for a small business of being on the Internet include:

- You can have global reach from day one, without the bother of getting a passport, a visa or turning up at an airport.

- You can extend your working time to 365 days a year, 24 hours a day, without creating an enormous wages bill or imposing impossible demands on the few people you have who can deal with sales enquiries or handle customer support.

- Things can change very quickly in a small business. If you do business online you can make changes to your product and service offers or prices quickly and inexpensively and fine-tune your propositions.

- You can reduce human error by eliminating some stages in each transaction. The more times a piece of information is handled between a customer's enquiry and the order being fulfilled, the greater the chances are of something going wrong.

Read Ben Carter, Gregory Brooks, Frank Catalano and Bud Smith's *Digital Marketing For Dummies* (published by Wiley) to get a thorough insight into this vital aspect of marketing.

Promote your website by acquiring links on other commercial websites, using key words to ensure you can be found, and by promoting outside the Internet – feature your website address on all products and publications. Fill your homepage with regularly updated success stories, give discounts to first-time buyers and ask customers to bookmark your site or add it to their list of favourites on their browser. You could also try partnering with manufacturers and distributors in related business fields.

Deciding on content

The danger with producing content for websites is to fall into the trap of believing that because it costs virtually nothing to load your site up with copy, pictures, diagrams and videos, it's a good idea to do so. When it comes to marketing messages, less is best. Think through what you want website visitors to do as a result of arriving at your site – place an order, ask a question, gather more information, see a demonstration and so forth; and then produce the minimum clear content to achieve those goals.

Designing the website

You probably already have a basic website writing tool with your office software. If you use Microsoft Office you'll find free web design tools in the Publisher section of your software. Basic stuff, but it gets you up and running. For more on building a website for free, check out David Crowder's excellent *Building a Web Site For Dummies* (published by Wiley).

You can also find hundreds of packages from £50 to around £500 that, with varying amounts of support, help you create your own website. Take a look at these sites:

- **BT Broadband Office** (www.btbroadbandoffice.com/businesstoday/0,9737,cats-5528530,00.html) has dozens of articles on how to improve your website design.

- **Top Ten Reviews** (http://website-template-service-review.toptenreviews.com) provides an annual report on the best website creation templates rated by ease of use, help and support, value for money and a score of other factors. The best buy as I write this edition is a third of the price of the third ranking programme.

- **Web Wiz Guide** (www.webwiz.co.uk/kb/website_design) has a tutorial covering the basics of web page design and layout.

More expensive options come with access to an editor, hours of webmaster assistance per month, a domain name, hosting, email and more.

Good website design is essential to having a successful experience online. Even though broadband is fast becoming the norm, you should pay careful attention to *loading time* – that is, how long it takes the recipient's computer to download your data. If loading takes too long, people may leave without looking at your site at all and you may have lost an opportunity for a sale. The rules here are to use graphics rather than photographs, which take up too much memory, and keep the text short, sweet, legible and attractive. You can check your website's loading time at the search engine optimisation company 1-Hit's website: www.1-hit.com/all-in-one/tool.loading-time-checker.htm (I explain search engine optimisation in the later section 'Gaining Visibility').

Research shows that visitors have to be hooked within three clicks or they jump ship to a more user-friendly website. So clear signposting is essential, with a simple menu of options on every page and a link back to your homepage so visitors can get back to their starting point.

Information on your site needs to be fresh and informative. Nothing is quite so off-putting as being on the fastest method of global communication known to humanity and seeing an invitation to a seminar that's already taken place or a special offer that expired weeks ago. You can buy in a news feed covering topics related to your business such as finance, travel or politics, or just general news, to ensure that your front page is always busy and topical, without you having to do a single thing. Check out sites such as Yellowbrix (www. yellowbrix.com) that harvest hundreds of thousands of news articles every day from the most respected news sources and categorise them into topics covering virtually every industry.

Check out Bad Website Ideas (www.badwebsiteideas.com) to see how to avoid the biggest howlers, and in consequence how to get your website design right.

Using a consultant

Thousands of consultants exist who claim to be able to create a website for you. Prices start from £499 where a consultant tweaks an off-the-peg website package slightly to meet your needs, to around £5,000 to get something closer to tailor-made for you. The Directory of Design Consultants (www.design directory.co.uk/web.htm) and Web Design Directory (www.web-design-directory-uk.co.uk) list hundreds of consultants, some one-man or one-woman bands, others somewhat larger. You can look at consultants' websites to see whether you like what they do. Web Design Directory also has some useful pointers on choosing a designer.

If you're working within a set budget you could consider auctioning off your web design project. Make sure though that those who you offer the auction to are going to do the job that you need.Using People Per Hour (www.peopleperhour.com) you state how much you're prepared to pay with a description of the project and freelancers around the world bid under your price, with the lowest bidder winning.

Registering domains

Having an Internet presence means you need a *domain name* – the name by which your business is known on the Internet and that lets people find you by entering your name into their browser address box, such as example. com. Ideally, you want a domain name that captures the essence of your business neatly so that you'll come up readily on search engines and one that's as close as possible to your business name.

Domain names come in all shapes and sizes. Those such as '.com', exude an international / US flavour, whilst '.co.uk' implies a UK orientation. Charities usually opt for '.org', or '.org.uk' whilst '.net' or '.net.uk' are used by Network Service Providers. Businesses often use '.biz' but it doesn't really matter what domain you use, what you want is to be seen.

Some domains are restricted. For example '.ac.uk' is used by higher education institutes in the UK and '.gov.uk' is used by UK government departments.

If your business name is registered as a trademark you may (as current case law develops) be able to prevent another business from using it as a domain name on the Internet.

After you've decided on a selection of domain names your Internet service provider (ISP), the organisation that you use to link your computer to the Internet, can submit a domain name application on your behalf. Alternatively, you can:

- ✔ **Use Nominet UK** (www.nic.uk), the Registry for British Internet domain names, where you find a list of members who can help you register, though you can do so yourself if you're web aware.

- ✔ **Use a world directory of Internet domain registries** if you want to operate internationally, for example by using a .com suffix or a country specific domain. Check out www.internic.net and www.norid.no/domenenavnbaser/domreg.html.

- ✔ **Use a company that sells domain names,** such as Own This Domain (www.ownthisdomain.co.uk) and 123 Domain Names (www.123domainnames.co.uk), which provide an online domain-name registration service usually with a search facility so you can see whether your selected name has already been registered. Companies such as Altaire (www.altaire.com/domain_names) and Electric Names (www.electricnames.co.uk) have detailed domain name registration on their websites as well as offering a same-day registration service for prices between £10 and £25 per annum.

The IT and E-commerce section of the Business Link website (www.businesslink.gov.uk) has comprehensive up-to-date information on all aspects of getting your website up and running as well as complying with the latest regulations.

Selling Goods and Services

Everything from books and DVDs, through computers, medicines and financial services and on to vehicles and real estate are sold or have a major part in the selling process transacted online. Holidays, airline tickets, software, training and even university degrees are bundled in with the mass of conventional retailers such as Tesco that fight for a share of the ever-growing online market. The online gaming market alone has over 217 million users.

Not all business sectors are penetrated to the same extent by the Internet. According to Forrester (www.forrester.com), the Internet research company, although sales of clothing and footwear online is a multi-billion-pound business it only accounts for 8 per cent of total sales. Contrast that with computers where 41 per cent of sales occur online.

Using third party websites

Selling online may be a sound way into market, but you still have another option: tag along with someone else, much as you would if you were selling a product into a shop. That way you don't have to deal with the procedures of selling on the Internet that, aside from having your own website, require systems for showing and describing the goods and services on offer, as well as ordering payment and fulfilment facilities (these topics are the subject of the following sections).

The main advantages to setting up your own selling procedures are that you have greater control over where your products appear, which can be important to people passionate about their venture; and you get to keep the whole profit margin rather than sharing it with others in the channels of distribution. But in varying ways you could end up passing up to a quarter of your margin in this way. Setting up your own online sales operation requires several thousand pounds of investment up front and a continuing stream of investment to keep your systems up to date, much as a retailer would need new shop fittings.

The other way of getting your goods and services to Internet markets is to piggyback on established, ready-built e-tail platforms such as those run by **Amazon** (www.amazon. co.uk/gp/seller/sell-your-stuff.html) or **eBay** (http://pages.ebay.co.uk/businesscentre).

Building a store front

Okay, so you've decided to take the plunge and set up your own shop front. If you were selling from a shop you'd set out your window display and have a basket for customers to drop their shopping into prior to checking out and paying. Your online store has much the same features with buttons and boxes around your order page allowing customers to select colours, sizes and quantities, place their order, pay and track the progress of their delivery. You need to decide what you want your online store to do because with linkages to other services you can arrange payment, delivery and even stock re-ordering, all of which come at an increasing price eating into your profit margin.

You can choose between dozens of companies in the field such as Altcom (www.altcom.co.uk) and ekmpowershop (www.ekmpowershop.com), which have turnkey online shop fronts from £19.99 a month.

GoECart (www.goecart.com), now in its seventh edition, doesn't charge any listing or transaction fees and a merchant can open a store for around £3,150 a year. That fee includes all you need to handle up to 20,000 products: a shop front, trolley buying system, payment acceptance, fraud protection, compete order and stock management and web traffic statistics. GoECart also claims to have the most search engine friendly architecture.

Getting paid online

If you're going to trade on the Internet then some form of online payment such as a credit card merchant account is essential. An alternative is one of a new breed of businesses tailored expressly for the Internet. The leader of the pack is PayPal (www.paypal-business.co.uk). They claim to have 100 million accounts around the world and firms using their services get an average of 14 per cent uplift in sales.

Using PayPal you can in effect get a merchant account with all major credit and debit cards in one bundle without set up fees or a lengthy application process and start accepting payments within minutes. PayPal isn't free; you pay 20p per transaction and a sliding charge ranging from 3.4 per cent if your transactions amount to £1,500 in any month down to 1.4 per cent if sales are above £50,000 a month.

PayPal's Micropayments provides special rates for your low value transactions. For example, products selling for £2 incur a cost of 15p to receive payment.

eBay's international payments incur additional costs. PayPal charges a standard cross-border fee of 1 per cent and a foreign currency conversion fee of 2.5 per cent.

RBS WorldPay (www.rbsworldpay.com), Click and Buy (www.clickandbuy.com) and Durango (www.durango merchantservices.com) offer similar services.

You can keep up with all the various services by reading the Merchant Account Forum (www.merchantaccountforum. com), a free newsletter set up by Richard Adams who was so frustrated in his efforts to set up a merchant account for his first online business he decided to set up a site to review merchant accounts.

Fulfilling orders

You have two main options when it comes to actually getting products and services to customers after they've bought online. The simplest way is doing it yourself. Take the orders, clear the payment and despatch the product.

MetaPack (www.metapack.com), automates and improves customer delivery using one or more of 23 carriers that provide between them some 590 services. You detail what you're sending, to whom, when you want it delivered and any other particulars such as security and the MetaPack software recommends a solution and can do anything from printing off a despatch label to booking a courier pick-up. If you don't want the hassle of managing your own fulfilment you can ship your products to an outsourced fulfilment business that handles as much or as little of the process as you want. Contact companies such as International Logistics (www.ilgroup.biz) or you can search the UK Warehousing Association's membership database (www.ukwa.org.uk), where you can look for a company in your area by specific tasks such as garment hanging, order picking, shrink wrapping and cold storage.

Amazon (https://services.amazon.co.uk/services/ fulfilment-by-amazon/features-benefits/index. html) has its own fulfilment service. When you include the cost of overhead such as warehouse costs, packing supplies, postage and labour, dealing with customer service enquiries and returns handling, letting Amazon do the job may actually be a cheaper option than doing it yourself. Amazon claims to be able to get a small electronic item through its entire system from stock held in its warehouse to cash in your bank for around £1.85.

Gaining Visibility

Unless the world that matters to you knows how to find your website, you're winking in the dark. The tricks of the trade start with ensuring that your first page (your *homepage*) is chock full of words and phrases that people put into their search pane and that Google, Yahoo! or any other search engine they're using can find. Start by brainstorming the way in which customers might start enquiring about your products or services, as well as important key words and phrases used in your industry. For example, if you're selling fire extinguishers, words such as *safety*, *protection*, *prevention* and *equipment* are probably at least as important to include in your opening text as phrases such as 'Synthetic aqueous film – forming foam agent capable of fighting class A and B fires'.

Getting into search engines

Optimising your website*Search engine optimisation* (SEO) for short, is the best way to be sure of getting listed appropriately in a search engine.

First make a list of the words that you think a searcher is most likely to use when looking for your products or services. For example, a repair garage in Penzance could include keywords such as *car*, *repair*, *cheap*, *quick*, *reliable*, *insurance*, *crash* and *Penzance* in the homepage to pull in searchers looking for a competitive price and a quick repair. As a rule of thumb for every 300 words you need a key word or phrase to appear between 10 and 15 times. Search engines thrive on content so the more relevant content the better.

You can use products such as that provided by Good Keywords (www.goodkeywords.com), which has a free Windows software programme to help you find words and phrases relevant to your business and provides statistics on how frequently those are used. Good Keywords also has several additional filters and tools to help you refine your key word lists, but those come at a price, as you might expect. Expect to pay upwards of £63.

Search engine algorithms also like important, authoritative and prestigious terms. So although you may not be able to boast 'by Royal Appointment', if can get your press releases quoted in the *Financial Times*, your comments included in postings on popular blogs or your membership of professional institutes and associations into your homepage, your chances of being spidered rise accordingly.

Another way to gain visibility is to search out other websites with which you can swap links for free. For example, you may be able to persuade a company selling marine insurance to put a link on its site to your boat-selling website in a reciprocal arrangement. This probably only works with other small local businesses that have relatively little traffic to their websites. Still, you're not after volume but value. If another site has high-quality traffic with a strong need for your wares, this kind of arrangement may be worth the effort. Such relationships are known as *affiliate marketing*, which is new speak for a kind of finder's fee.

A variation of the affiliate marketing route is to go for banner advertising on sites that you can't get onto for free. You could even sell advertising yourself, but you need to prove a substantial volume of visitors to your site first. A number of online UK business directories exist, such as UK Business Directory (www.business-directory-uk.co.uk) and Free

Index (www.freeindex.co.uk), offering free listings to UK businesses and companies in exchange for a link from your company website linking to their directory.

That, I'm afraid, is the end of the free lunch. Everything else in the visibility business costs money. You can pay to be listed on a search engine or you can 'buy' your way up the list so that you appear in the first page of any search for your business sector. The following sections consider each option.

Using a submissions service

You can build words into your website that help search engines find you, but you can also go to a professional whose job it is to move you up the rankings. Submission services such as those provided by Submit Express (www.submit express.co.uk), Rank4u (www.rank4u.co.uk) and Wordtracker (www.wordtracker.com) have optimisation processes that aim to move you into the all important top ten ranking in key search engines.

Payment methods vary. For example, Rank4u has a no placement, no fee deal where you pay only after it's achieved the positioning you want. 123 Ranking (www.123ranking.co.uk) has optimisation packages aimed at small and new businesses for from $299 per annum. Search Engine Guide (www.search engineguide.com; go to Search Engine Marketing) has a guide to all aspects of search engine marketing.

Paying for placement

If you don't want to wait for search engines to find your website you can pay to have your web pages included in a search engine's directory. That won't guarantee you a position; so, for example, if your page comes up at 9,870 in Google's list then the chance of a customer slogging his way to your page is zero. The only way to be sure you appear early in the first page or two of a search is to advertise in a paid placement listing. Major search engines such as Google AdWords (http://adwords.google.co.uk), Yahoo! Search Marketing (http://searchmarketing.yahoo.com) and Microsoft adCenter (https:adcenter.Microsoft.com) invite you to bid on the terms you want to appear for, by way of a set sum per click.

Don't forget to submit the URL of your website domain name to search engines and re-register on a regular basis. Check on the search engine websites for the section headed 'Submit your site'. Submitting to each search engine repeatedly is time consuming but the process can be automated using some URL submission software such as that provided by WebPosition (www.webposition.com) or Web CEO (www.webceo.com) for between £95and £252 These programmes not only ensure your entry in search engines is kept up to date but also provide tips on improvement and tools to report on your search engine ranking.

If you have a compelling proposition you may persuade a search engine to offer you a 'pay-for-performance' deal, where they take a share of the profits you make from having extra visibility. One company working in this way is Highposition. net (www.highposition.net/pay-for-performance. html). *Digital Marketing For Dummies* provides an excellent primer on this complex subject.

Checking out competitors

To get some idea of what to include and exclude from your website check out your competitors' websites and those of any other small business that you rate highly. You can also get some pointers from the Web Marketing Association's Web Award (www.webaward.org). Take a look at the Winners section where you can see the best websites in each business sector. Also check out The Good Web Guide (www.thegood webguide.co.uk), whose site contains thousands of detailed website reviews.

You can keep track of how many times your competitors change information on their websites by using the services on offer from companies such as Update Patrol (www.update patrol.com) or WebSite-Watcher (www.aignes.com).

Don't get into the habit of constantly changing the fundamental layout of your website. Customers may wonder if it's still you that's running the show! Customers expect consistency as well as currency when they come to your website.

Tracking traffic

A wealth of information is available on who visits your website: where they come from in terms of geography, search engine and search term used; where they enter your website (homepage, FAQs, product specifications, price list, order page); and how long they spent in various parts of your website. That information is aside from the basic information you automatically receive from orders placed, enquiries made or email contacts.

You can use visitor data to tweak your website and content to improve the user experience and so achieve your goals for the website. For example, you may find that lots of visitors are entering your website via a link found on a search engine that takes them to an inappropriate section of your site, say the price list, when you want them to start with the benefits of your product or success stories. By changing the key words on which your website is optimised, or by putting more visible links through the site, you can drive traffic along your chosen path.

Part IV
The Part of Tens

'My friends on the dock helped me
with the slogan.'

In this part . . .

You probably have a file somewhere marked 'Miscellaneous', which contains all the information you know you're going to find really useful *one day*. You can think of this part as tips, cautions, and suggestions that will help you talk to the right people before you start up, whilst steering clear of the worst no nos.

Chapter 14

Ten Pitfalls to Avoid

In This Chapter

▶ Making sure that you have the right skill base

▶ Keeping track of key financial data

▶ Staying out of the failure statistics

Difficult times, such as those that occurred 2008–2010, can cause even the biggest and apparently most established firms to hit the buffers. After all, Lehman Brothers survived the 1929 depression and Woolworths had put in some time on almost every high street in the UK, yet both were swept away in the recent downturn.

Some 400,000 small businesses close down each year in the UK and over half of those closures occur in the first year of trading. Although not all the closures come under the heading of home-busting events, no one likes to have a personal failure on their hands, even if it doesn't wipe them out financially.

This chapter lists the main problems that cripple most small businesses that have to shut their doors in the first year or so.

Knowing Too Little

Running your own business calls for a well-rounded range of expertise. In the early morning you may have to be coach and trainer to a new employee, by mid-morning – coffee-break time in big business parlance – you can be negotiating with the bank for an extra line of credit, at midday you may be drafting a marketing strategy and the early afternoon can involve looking for suppliers for a new product you're thinking of launching. The late afternoon may find you delivering a rush order to a key customer, followed by a quick shifty around a competitor's premises and a couple of possible premises for you to move into if you grow as planned. The evening is devoted to drafting a job advertisement and a leaflet, leaving the weekend to get the books up to date and the VAT return done.

Take time out before you start your business to brush up on the range of skills you're going to need. More opportunities now exist than ever before for education and training, at every level, in the small business and management field. You don't require any formal academic qualifications for most of the courses and costs are generally modest. In certain cases, participants may be eligible for grants or subsidised training. The bulk of the activities are concentrated in universities and colleges throughout the UK.

Find a course for yourself or employees through these websites:

- ✔ The Skills Funding Agency (http://skillsfundingagency. bis.gov.uk) has a mission to ensure that people and businesses can access the skills training they need to succeed in playing their part in society and in growing the economy. The website includes advice on selecting a training programme and a directory of training providers using their impartial Skills Brokerage service. They aim to help employers and employees identify the best value for money, which may mean finding training that is partially or wholly funded by the Government.

- ✔ The Learning Directory (www.learndirect-advice. co.uk/providers) is the Government-funded national database of learning opportunities containing information on approximately 900,000 courses from more than 10,000 providers in the UK.

However, a growing number of opportunities are arising for the less mobile to take up some form of home study in the business field in general, and small-business opportunities in particular. With the growth of the Internet, British entrepreneurs may now find it practical and worthwhile to get their learning experience from virtually any part of the world.

Being Overly Optimistic about the Market

Business starters are, by nature, optimistic. You have to be to overcome the hurdles, both natural and man-made, that appear in your path. But the one area you can't afford to be over-optimistic about is the market itself. That's the one thing you can't change. You can replace people, you can improve products and you can find money or new premises. But the raw ingredient of any business, the potential market, is a given that you can't easily change. True, big businesses talk grandly about educating the market to appreciate their wonderful product or service, but educating markets calls for deep wallets and long time horizons, both in short supply in the small-business world.

 Take care not to develop the 'iceberg syndrome'. Don't believe that the small number of customers you can see is a sure indication of the great mass of other customers lying hidden below the water-line just waiting for you to sell to them. Believing that customers are simply waiting to be sold to and that competitors are either blind or lazy is a fundamental mistake.

Underestimating Start-up Time

Everything in business seems to take longer than you think. Premises take ages to find and even longer to kit out and be ready for use. If you start up before you're ready, customers may well be disappointed and rush around sharing their displeasure.

 Make a chart showing the key tasks that you have to carry out before you can start up your business in the left-hand column, with the timescale in days, weeks or months, as appropriate to your business, across the top of the chart. In the right-hand column show who's responsible for each task.

Draw a bar between the start and finish date for each key task, showing how long the task should take. Some of the tasks will overlap others and some will depend on the successful completion of earlier tasks. For example, you can't install the oven in a restaurant until you've found the premises and signed the lease. You can, however, research oven suppliers and negotiate the price and delivery. Use the chart to monitor progress and take corrective action as you go.

Spending Too Much at the Start

New businesses should be lean and mean. Don't spend too much on fixtures, fittings and equipment too soon. People with a background in big business often start with extravagantly high standards. They expect the latest computer equipment, broadband Internet access, colour photocopier and cappuccino maker close to hand, and to sit in an executive-style office from the outset. You have to spread these overheads across the products/services that you sell and you can lose your competitive edge by being too expensive.

Mistaking Cash for Profit

The cash that flows into the business hasn't had any of the automatic deductions knocked off it, as has a pay cheque from an employer. So the money that comes in is *gross* cash flow. It may be real cash, but it's not really yours, or at least not all of it is yours. You may be tempted to use this cash to maintain your living standards, but don't yield to it. When the bills come in – from the suppliers, for National Insurance, for VAT – as they inevitably do, you may be stuck for the cash to pay them. Her Majesty's Revenue and Customs puts more businesses into liquidation than anyone else.

Maintain a cash-flow forecast on a rolling quarterly basis. In that way you always have a one-year view of what's likely to happen to the cash in the business. Use the cash-flow projection to anticipate peaks and troughs in your cash flow.

Use a spreadsheet and either write the program yourself or use the template that comes with your accounting software.

Manual cash-flow systems are inefficient and discourage regular updates. On the other hand, spreadsheet updates are simple, efficient and free of arithmetical errors, at least.

Choosing the Wrong Partner

A partnership is to business life what a marriage is to the rest of your life – a long-term, all-pervading relationship that spills over into and affects everything you do. Partnerships are complicated affairs, relying as much on chemistry as on personal attributes, skills or knowledge. Just as you should never embark on a marriage without a few months of dating at the very least, you should find a way to test out a partnership before you formalise the relationship.

Take on a project together that involves using the skills and expertise you hope your prospective partner brings to the business. If you want the person to do the buying, for example, go to a trade show together, preferably one that involves a couple of days' travelling to and from the venue. Watch her at work talking to exhibitors and opening up negotiations. Get her to meet others involved with your business – your spouse, bank manager, key clients; in fact, anyone who knows you well – and get their reaction.

The big factor to keep in mind is that a business partnership is likely to last longer than the average marriage. So if you can't face that, don't start a partnership.

Ignoring Accounting

Many owner-managers see accounting as a bureaucratic waste of time that they only carry out to keep the tax authorities off their backs and make it easier for those authorities to carve a deeper trough in their hard-won profits. Although you can have some sympathy with that point of view, you can't condone it. For too many new businesses their first year's accounts are also their last. By the time they really know what's going on it may be too late to put things right.

Forgetting Working Capital

Most business starters can work out how much the big-ticket items cost – computers, vehicles and office furniture, for example. But they often forget to allow for the recurring items such as money owed by customers, stock in trade and 'invisible' items such as insurance. To make matters more complicated, these items often have time lags associated with them. A customer who owes you money has to be financed until she pays up, as do your raw materials until you can turn them into saleable product that's been delivered and paid for. These items constitute a business's working capital, and the more successful you are, the more of a problem working capital becomes.

Think about it. The first thing that happens when you get a new big order is you need the ingredients or raw materials to put it together. Your suppliers expect payment within 30 days, or perhaps even on a pro forma basis (cash with delivery) in your early months of trading. But the snag is that you have to work up your product using bought-in raw materials, which may take weeks or months, and then wait for months for payment. In the meantime you're hung out to dry with a growing need for working capital. The paradox is that nearly as many businesses go bust with the sales curve going up as with it going down. The technical term for this is *over-trading* and the cure is to allow for it in your business plans and make sure that you have sufficient working capital in place to survive.

Having No Clear Competitive Advantage

You or your product or service has to have something unique about it that makes you stand out from your competitors. It may be something as obvious as being open later or longer. Or it may be a policy such as the John Lewis Partnership's 'never knowingly undersold' message. Whatever your unique selling proposition is, communicate it effectively.

Choosing the Wrong Location

Where you conduct your business and how much rent you pay are vital factors. Don't be tempted to take premises just because the rent is cheap – a reason usually exists for this, such as few customers passing that route or poor transport links, making the premises difficult for employees and suppliers to get to.

Equally, don't take on an expensive town-centre site if your turnover is unlikely to cover your outgoings. Your market research should help you identify a suitable location.

Chapter 15

Ten People to Talk to Before You Start

In This Chapter

▶ Identifying all the key people who can help you get started

▶ Leveraging your network of contacts to maximum advantage

▶ Taking advantage of free advice

▶ Getting the lowdown on what people really think are your strengths and weaknesses

*S*tarting up a business can be a lonely endeavour, but you don't have to do it all on your own. Hundreds of people, some just a few feet away, can give you useful insights into your skills and attributes, and they may even have a useful perspective on the viability of your business idea.

Speaking with Your Spouse

Your spouse may not know a great deal about your great business idea, but you can be sure she knows a lot about you. Your spouse can remind you of your weaknesses and help you play to your strengths. She also needs to be prepared for the long hours and lack of holidays that are sure to feature in the early months and years as you get your business established. This may mean that you need to re-divide the existing sharing of household and family tasks, such as taking children to school, family visits and painting and decorating, to reflect the new balance of work. That may prove contentious, so talking the issues through at the outset may save conflict and arguments when time constraints really start to bite.

The money put into the business is going to have an impact on the money available for other areas of family expenditure, so your spouse also has to be comfortable with the financial commitments you're taking on. Unlike most other investments you may have made – on houses and cars, for example – you can lose all the money you put into a business irrevocably.

One would-be entrepreneur who set out to open a bookshop was reminded by her partner how she disliked dealing with the general public. She loved books and delighted in visiting book fairs and auctions. But when reminded that essentially the job entailed opening and closing a shop six days a week, her enthusiasm level took a dive. Better take a dive before you start up than have your cash take a dive a few weeks afterwards.

If you're thinking of taking up some franchises – Chemical Express (www.chemicalexpress.co.uk), for example – then you may be asked to bring your partner along to the initial interview even if she's not going to be involved in the running of the business. Chemical Express wants to make sure that your partner is backing you 100 per cent, both practically and emotionally.

Making Use of Your Professional Network

The people in your network of associates have large chunks of the knowledge you need to get your business successfully launched. The ability to create and maintain strong professional relationships is an important key to business success. Networking is a vital business skill that lets you cultivate lasting business relationships and create a large sphere of influence from which you can find new clients, contacts, referrals and opportunities.

You can use a network for just about anything, from finding a new supplier to getting introductions to overseas sales agents. You can find a reliable bank manager, a new accounting software package or a great venue for your next business meeting. Your network contacts, unlike almost everyone else in the business world, are usually unbiased and authoritative. You should make few major decisions without recourse to network contacts.

Benefiting from Entrepreneurs Who Started a Similar Business

People like nothing more than talking about themselves and their successes. Obviously, if someone thinks you're going to steal her customers, she shuts up like a clam. But if the business you plan to start is unlikely to infringe on their sphere of activities, most established entrepreneurs are only too happy to pass on some of their hard-earned tips.

First establish that you're not going to tread on the entrepreneur's toes. For example, if you plan to start up in the same line of business 30 miles away, you have little chance of causing each other much trouble. You may even be able to open a shop at the far end of the same town as a competitor without doing the entrepreneur any serious damage.

Use your common sense as to whom to approach and, to be on the safe side, double the distance that you feel is a safe gap between you.

You may also find someone who's had a business failure in the field you plan to start up in and is prepared to talk. You can find such people by scouring the press or talking to trade associations and other operators in your sector.

Don't take everything entrepreneurs say, even the most successful ones, as inevitably right. The five businesspeople who comprise the dragons in the BBC programme *Dragon's Den*, with a combined personal wealth nearing £1 billion, can reasonably be expected to know a thing or two about new business ideas. Andrew Gordon presented to them his invention for propping up wobbly table legs and they unreservedly gave it the thumbs down. Despite being ripped to shreds as a concept, his stabletable (www.stabletable.co.uk), eight plastic leaves pinned together, has sold in industrial volumes on the Internet. The device earned the 34-year-old in excess of £500,000 in his first year and is now being sold in packs of 25 for use in restaurants, hotels, pubs and cafes throughout the world. Andrew is an inspiration to all would-be business starters whose ideas receive a less than rapturous reception from fellow entrepreneurs.

Events can be a valuable route to extending your business network. Useful organisations include the following:

- ✓ The Glasshouse (`http://theglasshouse.net`), founded in 1998, holds networking events bringing entrepreneurs, financiers and business advisers across all sectors together to provide support, encouragement and inspiration to would-be business starters.

- ✓ The Junior Chamber International United Kingdom (`www.jciuk.org.uk`) is a personal development and networking organisation for the under-40s. It's part of the global Junior Chamber International (JCI), which has over 250,000 members in 100 different countries.

- ✓ Networking4business (`www.networking4business.com`) organises business-to-business networking events that enable you to meet many other businesspeople without any commitment and in a relaxed, informal atmosphere.

Spending Time with a Friendly Banker

Despite having had a bad press during the credit crunch, these guys and girls have a lot to offer other than oodles of cash (or not!). Bankers see a lot of different people about a lot of different businesses. You can draw on their wide range of knowledge and experience. Your banker may be familiar with your type of business or the location you're interested in, or have advice on different financing options.

Start by talking with a bank manager you don't want to borrow money from. Begin the conversation by asking for advice, rather than money. Only when you've convinced yourself that your proposition is an appropriate one for a bank should you make a pitch.

Tapping into Your Local Enterprise Agency Director

Over 1,000 business experts are sitting in a local office somewhere near you just waiting to offer advice, help, encouragement and support to anyone thinking about starting a business. The even better news is that the services they provide are either free or low cost. Enterprise Agencies have been around for 25 years and are an initiative started by big business to help small business. Make sure that you grab your fair share of this expertise.

Communicating with Your Current Boss

Talking to your boss about anything other than the job in hand is always a tricky decision. Talk about your entrepreneurial vision too soon and you may find yourself sidetracked for promotion and pay rises and perhaps even first in line for the next downsizing event. Leave it too late and your boss may see your action as disloyalty at best and betrayal at worst.

If you plan to start up in the same line of work and possibly even try to take some key accounts with you, then you'd better talk to a lawyer rather than your boss. But if the climate is right and you can talk to your boss, a number of valuable things may happen. You boss can be a source of investment capital, a business partner or a useful resource for business advice and contacts.

Calling Your Colleagues

Those you've worked alongside over the years have formed a view about your talents. Your spouse has seen you after work, but they've seen you at work. If they don't know your strengths, weaknesses, foibles and desires, then no one does. At worst they may tell you that you're barmy and explain why; at best they may join you in the venture or invest their hard-earned savings in your business.

If you were thinking about taking on a partner, then casting your eye around your colleagues is a good place to start looking. Remember, it cuts both ways. Although they may know a lot about how you perform at work, you know as much about them.

Bringing in Your Best Friend

On the assumption that your best friend isn't your spouse, then she represents someone else who should be able to tell you whether you're the right sort of person to start up the particular business you have in mind. You can start out by asking your friend to review your skills and knowledge inventory and so provide a valuable crosscheck on your self-assessment. In fact, you should always find someone who knows you really well to go through this and the business idea-evaluation process. Unfortunately, everyone's capacity for self-deception is unlimited, and you shouldn't miss any opportunity for a reality check.

Reporting to an Accountant

You need an accountant in any event. However, don't miss out on making the maximum use of as many accountants as possible when researching to establish your business. Take all the free advice you can get, because most accountants give you a free first meeting in the hope of signing you up as a client.

Pump the accountants as much as you can for any tips, pointers or advice on the business you have in mind.

- ✔ Accountants are the first port of call for any entrepreneur seeking help and advice, ahead of bank managers, small firm advisers and business associates. As a consequence, they're the repositories of an enormous amount of information on every aspect of business, not just finance.

- ✔ Accountants draw an increasing amount of their revenue from non-accounting tasks, and some even make more money from providing general business advice than they do from auditing.

- ✔ Most accountants are sole traders or in small partnerships operating in much the same way as you plan to do when you set up your business. So unlike bank managers, who all work in large organisations, accountants can identify with your problems and concerns.

Plugging into a Business Angel Network

Business angels have some attractive attributes. They aren't as risk averse as venture capital firms; they act more quickly, putting up money in weeks rather than months; and they aren't so fussy about your pedigree. But when it comes to giving a helping hand, they're absolute stars.

Index

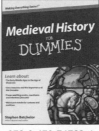
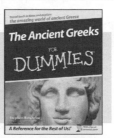